Parenting Boys

How to Develop Your Child Socially

(Your Adventure Guide to Parenting)

Jon Thompson

Published by Rob Miles

© **Jon Thompson**

All Rights Reserved

Parenting Boys: How to Develop Your Child Socially (Your Adventure Guide to Parenting)

ISBN 9781990084430

All rights reserved. No part of this guide may be reproduced in any form without permission in writing from the publisher except in the case of brief quotations embodied in critical articles or reviews.

Legal & Disclaimer

The information contained in this book is not designed to replace or take the place of any form of medicine or professional medical advice. The information in this book has been provided for educational and entertainment purposes only.

The information contained in this book has been compiled from sources deemed reliable, and it is accurate to the best of the Author's knowledge; however, the Author cannot guarantee its accuracy and validity and cannot be held liable for any errors or omissions. Changes are periodically made to this book. You must consult your doctor or get professional medical advice before using any of the suggested remedies, techniques, or information in this book.

Upon using the information contained in this book, you agree to hold harmless the Author from and against any damages, costs, and expenses, including any legal fees potentially resulting from the application of any of the information provided by this guide. This disclaimer applies to any damages or injury caused by the use and application, whether directly or indirectly, of any advice or information presented, whether for breach of contract, tort, negligence, personal injury, criminal intent, or under any other cause of action.

You agree to accept all risks of using the information presented inside this book. You need to consult a professional medical practitioner in order to ensure you are both able and healthy enough to participate in this program.

Table of Contents

INTRODUCTION 1

CHAPTER 1: NURTURING SMARTNESS 2

CHAPTER 2: FINANCIAL STRAIN ON SINGLE PARENT HOUSEHOLDS 13

CHAPTER 3: HOW TO BE THE "ULTIMATE" PARENT 17

CHAPTER 4: CUSTODIAL VISITS 26

CHAPTER 5: THE MAGICAL MESSAGE 31

CHAPTER 6: CONFLICT RESOLUTION 42

CHAPTER 7: GOALS, SUCCESSES AND FAILURES - TEACH YOUR CHILD HOW TO COPE WITH THEM 49

CHAPTER 8: AN OVERVIEW OF THE CHILD GROWTH AND DEVELOPMENT STAGES 55

CHAPTER 9: FAMILY TIME 73

CHAPTER 10: REASONS FOR SUICIDE 79

CHAPTER 11: THE SIX STEPS OF DISCIPLINE 83

CHAPTER 12: THE GOOD AND THE NOT-SO- GOOD PARENT 92

CHAPTER 13: 10 QUICK TIPS TO DEAL WITH TODDLER TANTRUMS 99

CHAPTER 14: HOW TO GET YOUR CHILD TO TALK ABOUT THEIR FEELINGS 106

CHAPTER 15: POSITIVE DISCIPLINE WITH CLEAR EXPECTATIONS INSTILL GOOD BEHAVIOR 111

CHAPTER 16: HELP THEM HAVE CONFIDENCE 116

CHAPTER 17: COMMUNICATION BASICS FOR PARENTS. 121

CHAPTER 18: EVERY SECOND MATTERS 128

CHAPTER 19: TIPS FOR BUILDING RESPONSIBILITY 131

CHAPTER 20: PAVLOV'S DOGS 138

CHAPTER 21: PREPARING YOURSELF 144

CHAPTER 22: SMART KIDS ARE MOTIVATED 147

CHAPTER 23: THINGS YOU CAN DO TO PROTECT YOUR CHILDREN'S SKIN FROM THE HARSH SUN 157

CHAPTER 24: FOOD FLYING EVERYWHERE 163

CHAPTER 25: TIPS ON DEALING WITH PARENTHOOD 167

CHAPTER 26: KEEPING COOL IN THE HEAT 176

CHAPTER 27: ENHANCING TODDLER DEVELOPMENT- FINE, GROSS AND VISUAL MOTOR EXERCISES 181

CONCLUSION.. **188**

Introduction

This book contains proven steps and strategies on how to understand why your kids have tantrums and how you can successfully manage them.

In this book you'll find out why kids have tantrums, what they use it for, and the many strategies and techniques that you can use to manage them. You will also learn to classify full blown major tantrums from minor episodes that can easily be managed. You will also learn the where and how tantrums are most likely to occur, what you can do to prevent an incident, and how you can manage the tantrum as it happens.

Thanks again for downloading this book, I hope you enjoy it!

Chapter 1: Nurturing Smartness

When nurturing a smart child's abilities, it is important that you focus on the child's preferences, and then build upon his interests and abilities. If you realize that your child has a certain skill or has a passion for a particular hobby, such as music, the first thing you need to do is provide opportunities for the child to nurture that ability at an early age. However, you do not need to make it something complicated like a Suzuki violin class while at the age of three. It can be something simple such as singing in the church choir or taking part in the community theater musicals. However, make sure you do not limit your child to this. It is imperative that you expose your kid to other options, such as playing an instrument. The idea is to provide opportunities for the child to nurture his/her abilities and interests no matter what they are. You also need to understand that even though your child may be exceptionally great in Math, you may find that he/she is also talented and interested in music and may actually enjoy playing a musical instrument. However, unless you give the child an opportunity to develop these abilities, these talents and skills will remain hidden and untapped.

On the other hand, while it is encouraged to nurture your child's interests at an early age, by no means are you allowed to enforce them onto your child. Conversely, even if you do not force your child to nurture his/her abilities, you should not allow them to quit on the way or before trying it. Most children whose parents have a high IQ tend to develop a similar mental ability. However, while genetics is thought to play a major role in this development, the environment in which the child is raised is also a significant contributor, in much the same way as the genetic hardwiring. The best thing you can do for your child in order to nurture their intelligence and enable him/her explore his/her other abilities is to provide an enabling environment. In most cases, several factors hinder the development of a child's abilities, including television and video games. In fact, studies have shown that about thirty percent of American children at the little age of two have television sets in their rooms and spend at least two hours everyday watching TV. This has led to slowed cognitive skills and reduced brain development time, which should be spent interacting with real people.

How To Make The Most Of Your Child's Time

When you think about it, most of the waking time your child spends is used up by technology. If your child is not sleeping, he/she is watching television, playing video games, on Facebook or Twitter or playing with some other electronic gadget. We have also not forgotten about the time they spent texting. While most of the time, we tend to make these allowances because we too are similarly addicted to technology, we need to understand that this can cause a significant shift in your child's destiny from an early age. Why, you may ask? While if utilized well, technology can benefit you and your family greatly; the downside is that if not used appropriately, then it would be more of a curse than a blessing.

Did you know that technology has been credited with setbacks in major brain development areas, leading to slow mental development and underdeveloped interactive skills? But, how can you shift this reality into something more constructive? How can you ensure that your child utilizes their time well in order to develop their abilities, both academic and other areas of life? This question is subjective, and depending on the interests of your child, you can apply different techniques for your child's intelligence development. First, you need to make that time by cutting back on the time spent on technology. In some cases, you may find that your child spends most of the time on books and such academic stuff. In that case, you need to make them understand the value of achieving in other areas of life without necessarily laying back on his/her studies. So how can we ensure that our children spend their time adequately? The only way we can do this is to find time so that our children can engage in different activities each day. How do you achieve this you may ask? By adequately teaching them how to manage their time well so that

Adequate Time management

Most people are unaware of this deficiency in their child's life, especially if the child is smart. After all, they assume, since a child is smart and naturally gifted, they already know how to manage their time. The truth is, just because your child portrays similar mental traits as Albert Einstein, does not mean that they have the necessary time management skills. In fact, this has been one of the most distinguishing elements between an all rounded achiever and a singularly smart kid. If you train your child how to manage their time well, he or she will gain the platform to concentrate on other areas of his/her time as well. I will share with you some effective time management skills that will set your child for success in the future from an early age. So where do you start?

Buy your child a calendar. The best way to start teaching your child how to manage their time well is by providing them with a calendar. This can be effective in ensuring that they keep up with events and activities everyday. You can then mark important holidays, events, and such important occasions such as birthdays for your child to remember. When this has being achieved, you can then proceed to schedule your child's day-to-day activities. Here, you can plan their activities for the day, from morning until evening when they are going to sleep. After school, you can post such commitments as sports practices, music lessons, Bible study, or scouts. These can be helpful in ensuring that the child does not only dwell on technology or, in this case, academics all the time. In fact, this is also a great way to utilize the child's time for social interactions with other peers in order to develop the much needed people skills. Moreover, it will get your child into an organized state, and will avoid future complications that arise out of isolation and lack of interaction skills. Of course, what better way to teach your kids on procrastination and the importance of planning than through a calendar?

Point of note: make sure you do not over schedule; otherwise, you will risk overburdening your child's young brain.

Nurture Their Sports Interests

The benefits of playing sports for a young child's mental development cannot be overemphasized. In fact, studies have shown that children who engage in at least one sport have a higher potential to succeed in academics than those who hide themselves in their rooms playing video games. Some of the complications associated with too much indoor time include deficiency in vitamin D, vulnerability to ADHD, weight related diseases and depression. However, the best time to nurture sports in your child is during his/her first years. The reason for this is quite simple; this is the time the brain is most flexible to absorb new information. If your child learns to balance between sports and education at an early age, chances are high that it will not be a major issue in the future.

A good way to start is by providing a child friendly playing space for your kid. Make sure that the area is free of any debris or hazardous substances that may harm your child while playing. When you go out to the park, let your child play freely and explore on his or her own. In addition, depending on where their interests lie, provide the necessary tools for them to explore their passions with. For instance, if you notice that your child loves playing on the beach, you may encourage their play by buying him/her a beach ball or something of the sort that will make them want to go to the beach even the more. Similarly, if your child has a particular interest in digging, you may buy him/her a bucket and a spade that will make them want to go to the beach even more. During your free time, you could also organize family boding time and involve your kids. Some of the activities you could take part in together include bicycling over the weekend, swimming, and rock climbing. It does not have to be something complex. Even a walk to the ice cream parlor instead of driving after school, or going to the kid's neighborhood entertainment area can be lots of fun. One of the benefits of engaging your kids in family bonding activities is that it helps stick in their mind that outdoor activities are meant to be fun, and not a chore.

You could also enroll your kid in some outdoor training classes such as badminton, skating classes, gymnastics, football or cricket classes, or even a sports camp; again, depending on their areas of interests. The best thing about engaging in outdoor couching is that it not only helps to develop your child's sporting skills, but also enables him/her tap into their energetic self and become more active. Another great way to encourage play in your child is to invite your friends over, particularly those with kids. You can then engage them in various games such as hide and seek or hop, skip and jump. You could also create a sports tournament with either the children or the whole family. This will help create a sense of friendly competitiveness, which will motive them to go outdoors and participate in the included games.

Chapter 2: Financial Strain On Single Parent Households

There are many reasons why single parenting is not a good idea. There are the obvious reasons, of money, time, and energy, and then there are reasons that people who embark on the road to single parenting without even considering. There seems to be a reckless abandonment for the emotional well-being of children, kids and teens. There is no crime in being low income however; there is something to be said about an impoverished population of single women that has resulted from choices that were lacking consideration for all parties involved.

When single parents raise children, the possibility of being raised in an impoverished environment is more of a reality. Statistically, parents that divorce are more likely to experience poorer conditions than when they were married – however, typically, the financial state is somewhat sustainable.However, younger women who have children out of wedlock at an early age and keep the baby run the risk of becoming impoverished.Most of these women will not further their education, and many of them will not even finish high school.With those two established qualities, their ability to secure a job that can offer them advancement and opportunity is minimized or eliminated altogether.Many of these young women will embark on a lifetime of government assistance and food stamps as their only means of financial support.

Raising a child, or children – which often happens in these situations – with extremely limited financial support is a huge burden and problem for single parents.These parents never become self-reliant or fully independent financially, and statistics further show, neglect among the children, and the cycle typically repeats itself.

There is a huge disadvantage for single parents when it comes to money and income.The likelihood of getting ahead is often nonexistent.However, unfortunately, most single parents do not consider the ramifications of living at extremely low financial levels.School districts are typically zoned and most of the times, affordable housing and homes are in a district or part of town where low-income households are high.The majority of these households will have their children enrolling in the same school system, and unfortunately, based on statistics, the outcome is not good.

The majority of these single parent households are dealing with survival of being poor.Whether they are working or receiving government assistance, there is monumental financial stress that a struggling single parent will endure.Of course, single parents are not the only people who run the risk of being financially burdened; however, couples can work together, and rely on each other to improve the situation.But options are limited for the single parent.Time is restricted, opportunity is limited and ability to earn extra income revolves around the needs of the child.

Financial hardship is one of the many reasons that single parenting is not a good idea.Meeting the needs of kids and moving in a direction that is financially sustainable is a part of parenting.When the burden of finances is an issue, the stress can be overwhelming resulting in other negative impacts on the children.Single parenting should be thoroughly thought through and all options heavily and highly considered.

Chapter 3: How To Be The "Ultimate" Parent

We all know what a bad parent looks like: intolerant, constantly critical, more interested in their own affairs (in both senses of the word) than in the needs of their children. But what does it take to be a good parent? What does it take to give your children the very best start to life that you possibly can?

In the 1960's John Bowl by did a lot of work looking into the effects of parenting on children. In those days he coined the term "good-enough parenting". His thesis was that provided you avoided the sins of "bad" parenting, you were doing okay, and your children, with their own natural resilience, would also do okay. So is that all there is to it? Or are there things that you, as a parent, can do to be more than just a "good enough" parent. Can you, indeed, be a "super parent", even the "ultimate" parent? Or is that just a myth of the feminist movement?

Well, let's get one thing straight once and for all: No one is perfect. Try as you might, you will never be a "perfect" parent. You will never get it right every moment of every day for every year of your children's growing lives. Nor do you need to. In that sense, Bowlby's concept of "good enough" is very true. You do not need to be perfect. Your kids WILL survive. "Good enough" is good enough.

But, I suspect that you probably want more for your kids than just average. I strongly believe that there are things you can do, and attitudes you can adopt, that will give your children the very best start to life they could possibly have. And, at the same time, will actually make life easier and more fulfilling for yourself too. It is not a long list, but if you can manage the following, then I believe you have every right to call yourself the "ultimate" parent:

1) Recognize you are human. You cannot do everything, you cannot be everywhere, you cannot know everything. You will make mistakes. You also have your own issues, problems and hangups from your own past. That is all okay. The key to this game is not being perfect, but having the right attitude.

What is the right attitude? Being humble. Recognizing that you have much to learn (we all do) and being willing to be teachable and to learn from your mistakes. A sign of genuine maturity is being able to look back at your past, recognize the mistakes you made, and say "this is what I have learnt about myself, and what I need to work on changing in myself".

But there is a flip side to this. Constantly putting yourself down with an "I'm no good" attitude is just as bad as the "I have nothing to learn" attitude. Forgive yourself for your mistakes. Celebrate your successes. Look back to the past only long enough to learn from it, then set your sights forward, and press on in the directions YOU want to go. If you have any serious issues from the past, be brave enough to seek help and get over them.

2) Recognize you are playing a percentage game. We have all heard of them: the kids from the most abusive, deprived backgrounds who somehow manage to make huge successes of themselves. And the kids from the very best of families (as demonstrated by their siblings) who somehow go off the rails into drugs and crime.

The reality is that you, the parent, are only one factor in your children's upbringing. They are also subject to influence from the friends, other relatives, teachers, shop keepers, TV, magazines and, of course, their own genetic makeup. You cannot control all the variables. You might be the very best, the ultimate parent, and yet your kids turn out as failures. You might be the very worst, alcoholic and abusive parent, and yet your kids do fine. Nothing in life is guaranteed.

So you play the percentages. You know that if you beat your kids, they are more likely to turn out bad than good. So, on average, beating your kids is probably not a good idea. Using fair and consistent discipline probably produces better odds for a successful outcome - so do that instead.

You success as a parent is NOT determined by how well your children turn out. It IS determined by whether you did all you reasonably could to do the right things and make the right decisions for them, WITH THE KNOWLEDGE YOU HAD AT THE TIME. Maybe those decisions turn out to be the wrong ones. So be it. That does not mean you failed as a parent. But, if you were too lazy to get the facts, if you just took the easiest decision without thinking about the impact on your children, then, I believe, you have failed - even if it turns out that the decision was the right one!

3) Recognize your children are not the only things in your life. In this day and age we seem to be obsessed with the idea that the interests of the children come first, before anything else. I strongly disagree with that concept. Yes, me must consider the best interests of the child, but there are other things to consider too.

It may be, for instance, that taking a new job in a different city might be the best thing for your family - even if it means taking your child away from his school and friends.

By putting children first in everything we run the danger of creating a selfish, "me first" generation where they grow up believing that the world owes them a living. Sometimes children have to take second place - and that in itself is an important lesson about life. Yes, before making any decision consider its impact on the children. But, in the end, make up your own mind as to what would be best for the family as a whole.

4) Look to the long term. Raising children is a long drawn- out process. Have your long-term goals in mind. How do you want them to turn out as adults? What qualities and skills do they need to learn? What experiences do they need, along the way, to learn those skills and character traits?

Many times as parents we are faced with the choice of taking an easy, short-term quick fix, or a harder approach that will bear much more fruit in the long term. The TV is such a classic example of this. How easy is it, when the kids are playing up, to just switch on the TV as the electronic babysitter? A quick fix for the immediate hassle or rowdy kids. But how much better, in the long run, to spend a bit of time teaching them how to build a model, or sew a soft toy, or put together a jigsaw?

5) Look for the positives. Like you, your children will make mistakes. Forgive them. Correct them gently and move on. Always be looking for what they did right, not what they did wrong. Children crave their

parents' attention. Pay attention to what they do wrong, and they will do more of it. Pay attention to what they do right, and they will be eager to please you more.

6) Stick to your guns. Believe in yourself. If you are doing all the above, then you are well on the right track. There will be times when you make decisions and you get challenged on them, either by your children, or by others (such as interfering relatives). Unless there genuinely are new facts that you weren't aware of before, don't be swayed.
And don't be afraid to say no - to your children and your relatives - if that is the right thing to say.

Sure, your decision may turn out to be a bad one. That happens. Hindsight is 20-20. But far better to stick to your decision, than to be a plastic bag blowing about in the breeze. You children are watching you; watching how you deal with life, how you make decisions, how you cope with adversity, how you believe in yourself and stand up for yourself and your family. Be a good example for them.

Chapter 4: Custodial Visits

When my mom left, it left all kinds of questions in our minds. Moms don't usually go. It's usually the dad. My father was kind and explained that mom needed her career and that it was easier for us all to be together. If you explain the situations that occur which concern where the children will be, they can still anchor themselves. If they are taken from your home to hers without so much as a moment's notice, they feel uprooted and insecure.

When you agree custodial visits, make sure that the kids know what to expect. Remember that as far as the kids are concerned, you can only convince them that both parents love them by being as agreeable as possible to the terms of any custodial visitation order. Let the child know that you will miss him/her. That's important because your home with them is their base. They need to feel like they are coming home when the visitation is over and they also need to see their mom's house as being somewhere they visit, rather than being a second home.

One of the things that kids pick up on is when two parents cannot agree on what's acceptable and what's not. For example, if a child is expected to be in a bed at nine on school nights in one home, then the same rule should apply in the other. Kids will try to tell you all kinds of things, but you need to check out ground rules before visitations start so that both parents are working on the same lines. If they see favor from one parent, the children will very soon cotton onto being able to work situations to their own advantage. Agree with your ex-spouse that custody is conditional upon the children having the same rules so that their lives are not disrupted by rule changes every couple of weeks. That's really important.

You can be a wonderful dad and have all the rules in place when one visitation with your ex throws all of those rules out of the window. You may think this doesn't matter, but it really does. It means that the kids have found a loophole in the system and kids really will take advantage of it. I remember telling lies to my mom about being able to stay up late to watch a certain show. She should have had the common sense to know I was lying, but what happened was that when I was returned to dad, I felt anger that I could do something at her house that I couldn't do at home and took it out on my dad. If you let your kids get away with this, it's not just difficult for them. It's harder for you because the kids will have tantrums and the transition between visit and coming home will always be something you dread.

The way to do this is to draw up a schedule that covers just about anything a kid could be tempted to lie about. Do it in a fun way like a chart and get the kids to help so they don't see it as being authoritarian. Write down appointments they may have, times they go to bed, shows they watch on TV. They will think you are doing this so that the absent parent doesn't make them miss their favorite TV show, but what you are actually doing is setting the guidelines and asking the absent parent to work within those parameters so that the kids don't feel uprooted and uncertain about their lives when they go from one home to another.

It's always going to be hard to please everyone but if you cover the kids' needs on a chart, you also ensure that there is continuation and this helps to keep the kids in order and also helps them to have a regular pattern to their lives which they understand and which is done for their good.

The times when you may experience difficulty are going to be those times when you really do want to have your kids to yourself. As the parent who houses and looks after the kids, you should have priority. It doesn't always happen so be prepared for potential changes. For example, Christmas together may be what you planned, but it may also be what your ex planned. Make sure that you are always on the same page so that arguments don't occur especially at times when the family unit is of ultimate importance.

- The days to remember will be:
- Mother's day – She should see her kids
- Father's day – You should have the kids
- Children's birthdays – Compromises need to be made here
- Christmas – Again, compromise needs to be made

Think these out in advance and let the kids know because it makes a difference to their lives too. If you get a Christmas with the kids, make sure it's a really great Christmas for them to remember. Choose the tree together, get them to help with the decorations and even if you don't know how to cook cookies, have a go at it and let them join in. It's more about sharing than it is about achieving. Don't apologize because you can't do something than mom can. Do something different and equally as enjoyable and start to create Christmas customs of your own!

Chapter 5: The Magical Message

There is a man I know who was raised by what anyone would consider good parents.But even the best of parents make mistakes their children will have to overcome in their adult lives.This man's dad constantly told him, as he was growing up, not to be a 'blithering idiot.'Any time this man tread in a direction, of which, his father did not approve, his father would quip, "you're blithering."Would you be surprised to discover that as an adult, this man has had to fight for every ounce of his own self-confidence?Yet his father's intent was to warn, not to wound.His intention was to aide his son in avoiding what he deemed as mistakes.However, the results were less than satisfactory.

As parents, we often sow with the best of intentions, only to have our children reap the consequences.The road to hell is paved with good intentions.That hell is not some afterlife experience waiting to happen.Too often, in parenting, that hell is right here on earth.The vehicle we most often put the peddle to the metal in on the highway to hell is fueled by the things we, as parents, say.

Most of us were raised to say 'The Magic Word.'But 'please' is not the only word that conjures up the positive.Most every word we say has the ability to charm or jinx the person the word (or collection of words) is directed at.Unlike in fantasy stories, you do not have to mean what you say in order for your words to prove damaging.However, you do have to mean what you say in order for your words to empower.Is that fair?Probably not.But haven't you already taught your children that life is not always fair?The same applies to us.We, as parents, have to unlearn the 'dark magic words,' and practice using all of the other 'magic' ones. The process begins when we name our children.Reading the meanings of names can prove disconcerting.There are names that we can give our children that mean things like, 'from the bloody river,' and 'stranger; alien.'But names are to be a blessing, a hint at the future.I believe most parents name their kids for a reason.Do your children know what that reason is?If you have not already told them, now is the time.That reason may not be because you poured over what certain names mean until you found the perfect moniker.You might, for instance, have named your child after a favorite aunt or uncle.If that is the case, then tell your child what makes that relative such a special person and why you hope your child learns to emulate their namesake.Or maybe you chose a favorite place or people group (like Dakota,

Montana, Phoenix or Cheyenne).Something about that word drew you to it beyond the way it sounds.Explain this to your child so that her name will be a glory to her.Of course, if you chose the name Phoenix, do not be surprised if your child goes through a really difficult time that results in her becoming an incredible person.This is just one example of how a name can be a hint of your child's future.

Your child's name is only the beginning.Nicknames can be a blessing to a child as well.They can also be a curse.Calling your child 'rock star' can build them up, but don't complain when she gets a tattoo or a boyfriend with a neon green Mohawk.Every word you use about your child can build your child up, or tear your child down.Take, for instance, our dubious rap stars.Would you argue with me if I were to suggest that rap stars, well beyond other performers, promote derogatory messages toward women?In fact, do not rappers, in general, place all women into two profane categories?Therefore, is it any surprise that the women these rappers surround themselves with prove to be the very dregs of humanity these ignorant 'men' describe them as?It becomes an issue of the chicken and the egg.Were the girls already deviant, or did accepting the things the rappers say about them encourage their lack of positive behavior?Regardless of what science might prove in the matter, it is clearly evident with human eyes and human understanding that the girls who embrace the negative message these 'men' preach as if it were the gospel truth, flock to them like moths to a bug zapper.

This is simply further evidence as to why I believe that the words we say can have a dramatic impact on others.The whole 'sticks and stones' taunt is about as ignorant as the children using the phrase.Bones heal almost all of the time.In fact, bones typically heal stronger than they previously were at the site of the trauma.However, souls- especially young souls- do not always heal as well as we would like them to.Most psychological and spiritual wounds fester.The weapon most used to inflict these wounds on a soul is the tongue.Our tongues can either be scalpels, or daggers.Both blades pierce the flesh, but one aims to heal, while the other kills.

As parents, we brandish a very powerful version of this tool/weapon.What we say can remove cancer from our children's souls.Many a child, consistently wounded through teasing at school, has risen up to do great things because the two surgeons at home cut out the cancer of those wounds carefully and daily.But what we say can also stab our children right through their little hearts.The things we say to our children not only cut, but poison.The paradigm is as if the blades parents yield, when used the wrong way, are dripping with cobra venom.

The trick to wielding our tongues as tools of healing and building is to always frame what we say as blessings, not curses.For example, my daughter is as pretty as a princess.However, sometimes the sum of her actions is less than what is expected from one deemed royal.In those times I say to her, "You are as pretty as a princess on the outside.BUT don't think for one minute that daddy won't do what it takes to make sure that you are as pretty as a princess on the inside as well."It is simply a crafty way to say to her, 'you're better than this.'Our children need a reasonable expectation placed upon them.However, we must make sure that the expectation is to be the best 'her' she can be, not neighborhood superkid (that is unless she has been blessed with superpowers).

The issue goes beyond just what we say to how we say what we say.To illustrate this, say hello, while looking in a mirror, with raised eyebrows, hints of a smile, and a pleasant tone.Welcoming, isn't it?Now say hello again with your arms crossed, a proceeding sigh and a snotty tone.Feel like slapping yourself?Yet you verbalized the exact same thing: you said 'hello.'The truth is that sometimes how we say things tells more about what we are actually trying to communicate than the words we choose to use.I have heard many a parent saying the right thing to their child in the toy section of our local discount retailer.They might be telling the child that she didn't do her chores, or she had misbehaved or she got a note sent home from school that indicated a need for an attitude adjustment. But the tone, in which, the words are said screams out, 'you bleeping little bleep bleep bleep!'The only person that did not hear what the screaming parent said that way (with the exception of the guy collecting carts in the parking lot) was the parent herself.

Now I am not without understanding in this conundrum. I was raised in a house where a raised voice preceded discipline. But most of us have felt a form of this wrath and it typically did not lead to a proper change in behavior. In fact, most of us stood at the crossroads of rebellion in the wake of such decibel laden incidents. Though all the right things may be said here (albeit with an elevated volume), the way in which the words are said tears the child apart or forces the child to develop defenses that can (and will) impair every relationship the child ever has.

In our home we have discovered the power of the whisper. The voice that lets our children know that they have crossed the proverbial line is rather quiet. The beauty of this technique is that if our children misbehave in public, there is no risk of someone speed dialing Child Protective Services in order to bring them into line. How many times have we heard...

ah... someone else yell (at the top of her lungs) in the situation described in the previous paragraph, "you're embarrassing me!"?Ultimately, we must ask ourselves, 'who is embarrassing whom?'It is always a sobering and humbling realization to accept the fact that what we are doing is accusing our children of what we are actually doing.And, if in the future, our children are the ones who are at fault for perpetuating the public embarrassment, are they not simply following our poor example?

The best strategy we, as parents, can employ is a strategy where we do not allow our words, tone and body language to undo what otherwise would be effective parenting.Yet especially when we do everything right as a parent, our children have a free will and they will exercise that free will.Therefore, we must know the strategy necessary to bless our children when everything inside us wants to curse them.How do we deal with our children's ugly actions without being ugly ourselves?

Chapter 6: Conflict Resolution

Playing nice may be the very last thing you want to do after your divorce, particularly if you feel like you have been jilted or you loathe watching your ex flirt with his or her new romantic interest. In the long run, though, amplifying conflict will only amplify your own stress. This will make it harder to have a healthy relationship with your ex and it will feed the anger you already have surrounding your divorce. Know that your children will suffer immensely if you spend the rest of your life battling your ex. Remember, your children came from your ex, so when you insult your ex, you're insulting your children too.

Civil Communication

The first step towards communicating in a healthy way is to practice civil, clear communication tactics. Whether you're negotiating how the kids will spend Christmas or navigating a dispute over how to discipline your children, the rules are the same:

DO keep your communications clear, simple, and to the point. Rather than ranting about the importance of a regular bedtime or lodging allegations, state what the problem is and what you'd like for the solution to be. Then – and this can be hard, but is the key to nonviolent communication – solicit your ex's input. For example, try saying, "Johnny seems to have a lot of trouble concentrating in school when he stays up late. I think it works best if he's in bed by nine or so. What do you think?" This opens the channels of communication and immediately establishes that you're a team working together rather than a pair of adversaries.

DON'T make allegations. Instead, talk about yourself. Use statements such as, "I feel..." "I've noticed..." and "I'd like..."

DON'T attribute motives to your ex. Rather than telling him you know he's trying to undermine you, tell him you feel frustrated or concerned by a problem.

DO talk about the best way to communicate about your kids. Some exes have trouble communicating in person and prefer email or text. Others find that these approaches to communication increase conflict and misunderstanding. Find something you can both agree on.

DO schedule regular times to talk about the kids. Aim for a weekly catching up session or a monthly dinner to talk about any problems you're having.

DON'T get third parties involved. Trying to get your ex mother-in-law or neighbor to communicate with your ex on your behalf is a recipe for disaster. And definitely don't use your kids to relay messages to your ex; this is a form of emotional abuse.

Give a Little, Get a Little

If you want something from your ex, you need to be prepared to give something in return, because sacrifice is a two-way street. You'll gain lots of brownie points if you show you're willing to give something up first. For example, if you want extra time with your kids on Christmas, try saying, "Why don't you take the kids Christmas Eve? Could I then have them for an extra hour on Christmas?" Being willing to make adjustments to your custody agreement and to anticipate one another's needs, are keys for avoiding conflict. If your ex knows he can count on you to allow him to take the kids to a family reunion or funeral, he's much more likely to give you a few extra vacation days.

Benefit of the Doubt

You divorced your ex for a reason, so it's easy to see that reason in every single interaction. But don't assume that your ex is acting out of malice – even if you know she is. When there's a problem, try to find a positive emotion or motive you can attribute to your ex. For example, if she's keeping your child up way too late, try saying, "I know you love reading with Susie, and I think that's a big part of the reason she has such a strong vocabulary. But I'm concerned that when she stays up late reading, she is exhausted and cranky the next day. What can we do about this?" This is called a compliment sandwich. If you have a complaint, lodge it in between a compliment or two. Your ex will appreciate your recognition of her good qualities, and will be more likely to listen to your concerns.

Keeping the Kids Out of It

The cardinal rule of divorce is that your children should not even know if you and your ex are fighting. Your primary goal is to protect them from the conflict of divorce. This means following a few key rules:

Never say negative things about your ex to your children.

If you and your ex have different rules, don't tell your children that this is because you're a better parent.

Your kids should never be the messenger between you and your ex.

Don't ever let your children see you fighting. Be friendly and warm to your ex around your children. This teaches them good social and conflict management skills. It also helps them feel safe and secure.

Legal and Professional Help

Sometimes you can't resolve problems on your own, but this doesn't mean you have to go back to court. Some alternatives to hiring a lawyer and spending your time and money suing each other are:

Going to therapy together. A qualified professional can help you both discover your strengths and weaknesses and work more productively together.

Hiring a Parenting Coordinator. You could even incorporate one into your custody agreement. Parenting Coordinators are licensed professionals who help you talk through disputes. They also have the legal power to make minor alterations to your custody agreement.

Enlisting the assistance of a Guardian Ad Litem, a person who represents your child's best interests in your custody trial.

Going to mediation. This strategy is generally less conflict-laden than going to court, and gives you the opportunity to come to an agreement you can both live with.

Chapter 7: Goals, Successes And Failures - Teach Your Child How To Cope With Them.

In the previous chapter I've mentioned children's ability to take actions despite risks and the possibility of failure. But where does this ability come from? The answer is: from children's irresistible will. If a child's will is to walk, they won't stop trying until they learn how to do it. Unfortunately, it's often necessary to take actions or acquire particular skills that are essential in order to achieve the desired goal. However, these actions or skills are not encouraging in themselves. When you run a company, you need to be extremely persevere and systematic. That's why I think it's a good idea to teach your child these two character traits in advance. But how?

Setting goals.

If setting goals was easy, today's world would be definitely different. Nowadays, there are plenty of personal development experts who want to teach you how to set ambitious goals. Indeed, such a skill is highly useful, but you can prevent your child from reinventing the wheel, and foster the goal setting skill in them today.

Here, I'm giving you some examples how to do it:

1. Observe your child and use your observations.

I'm sure that your child used the goal setting and goal achieving skills more than once, unintentionally. This time try to observe what this process looks like. Maybe your child has eaten their vegetables so they could watch their favorite cartoon or eat a chocolate bar?Use this knowledge and talk to your child about what their emotions were when they'd been rewarded, and what their motivation was to eat the vegetables.

2. Begin with small steps.

Don't be overambitious, because you want to encourage your child, not discourage them. First, you need to set a small goal together, such as finishing a Lego building or a picture. It's the feeling of satisfaction with the achievement of this small goal that will encourage children to take more difficult challenges.

3. Create a plan.

The third example is particularly effective in older children. Ask your child for a list of 10 goals. Let them be, for example: a thing that you'd like to have, a thing that you'd like to be able to do, a thing that you'd like to happen, etc. Next, you establish a hierarchy of goals, starting with those that would influence your child's life most positively. Focus on the first goal, and create a list of steps essential to meet the goal. Encourage your child to take at last one of these steps right away.

4. Be thoughtful and alert.

Although children rarely are able to specify their goals, they quite often specify their wishes. On the basis of your child's wishes, try to create a plan to fulfill them.

Although not every plan will be actually used, and not all wishes will be worth creating such a plan, it's important to create a habit of setting and pursuing goals. For example: "I wish my doll had a swimming pool and beautiful dresses" - Establish the goal: what you will need to build a swimming pool, who will make the dresses, how to plan these tasks, etc.

5. A role model.

Children also learn by observation. Let your child be involved in your own goals. Show your child what you care about, and, most importantly, what effort you make to achieve your goals. It's essential that parents have their own goals, and their children know them.

Successes and failures - school gives bad example.

Unfortunately, school often makes children think that it's bad to make mistakes. Every mistake made in school results in a lower grade. On the other hand, making mistakes while being an entrepreneur teaches you a lesson. Like Napoleon Hill said: "Every adversity, every failure, every heartache carries with it the seed of an equal or greater benefit". By allowing your child to make mistakes, you give them the opportunity to seek new paths and problem solutions. Moreover, you give your child the opportunity to try these solutions in practice, and prevent your child from making similar mistakes in the future.

In practice:

When your child makes a mistake, don't act like a school teacher. Don't punish your child. Instead, discuss the cause of the mistake, how your child could've avoided it, what they could learn from the mistake, and what other actions they can take next time.What your child should repeat to themselves in case of a failure is: "Making mistakes is an opportunity to act in a better and more thoughtful way".

Does it mean that failures and mistakes won't happen again? No, it doesn't. But you don't have to wait for mistakes and failures to occur in order to draw conclusions. Teach your child to seek problems intentionally to foster the ability to create solutions.

In practice:

Encourage your child to tell you about current problems that concern them. Or ask your child about problems they've already coped with (for example, wet bread in a school sandwich, or inability to reach the highest shelf in the room). Have a brainstorming session. Let your child come up with as many problem solutions as they can. When creating problem SOLUTIONS instead of concentrating on the problems themselves becomes a habit, your child will solve future problems intuitively (and, admit it, those problems will be more and more serious with time). Moreover, your child will be able to reduce the fear of failure.

Chapter 8: An Overview Of The Child Growth And Development Stages

Newborn

At this stage, babies can spend sixteen hours a day sleeping and an enormous amount of changes are happening to them night and day. Most of a newborn's noises and movements are involuntary, no matter how directed and purposeful they seem. Newborns can be shocked by loud noises, and do respond to voices and sounds. They cry as their primary means of communicating with their parents, and parents should avoid seeing crying in the same context as they would with adults or older children. Newborns may use different types of crying for different needs, whether they need to be fed, changed, or put to bed. New parents usually soon come to recognize the difference. They should respond to their baby's cries in order to develop the bond all babies and parents need in order to cement the remainder of their relationships. Holding babies face to face, singing to them, walking with them, rocking them, and talking to them in a rich, soothing voice will all go a long way to help cement the bonding process.

Developing infant (1 month to 1 year old)

In the first three months of their lives, babies already begin to copy sounds, and develop more direct types of crying. They can recognize their parents' voices, smile at their parents responsively, and give feedback from social contact. Their range of motion and movements also increase, especially in their legs, as well as their responses to rhythms. They start taking in their environment with all five senses and exploring it as best as they can. One to three months old babies may start putting objects in their mouths, staring at their hands and playing with them, trace the movement of objects with their eyes, and rotating their hands while at rest. Between four and six months of age, babies start to develop their color and distance vision, which may make them more interested in their visual environments. Many of their newborn reflexes are gone by that point. They can start to pass objects between their hands. Within six months, babies can babble and copy sounds, make single-syllable utterances, laugh, giggle, and gurgle. The bubbly, happy popular image of babies is six months old at least.

Between four and six months, babies start to recognize familiar people and places, miss things, recognize certain commands and their names, and make certain gestures to communicate. Parents can do many things to encourage their baby's development at that this stage. Repeating the sounds your baby makes and smiling at them encourages them to keep on trying, and pressing onward to master language. Parents should spend some time each day placing their babies on the floor, in a nice blanketed sitting area, and playing with them. During this time, they can give them safe toys to look at and examine, play games of 'peek-a-boo' with them, and show them different brightly colored things and picture books. Parents can cuddle with their babies, dance with them while holding them, and introduce them to new sights and sounds. Introducing babies to new people helps give them a broader exposure. Games like 'peek-a-boo' help babies while they are still developing a sense of object permanence.

Comforting babies whenever they are sad only strengthens the bond further and helps them develop their own senses of empathy. By the age of ten to twelve months, babies have all but transformed from their new- born selves. They can do simple communication gestures like shaking their heads 'no,' copy certain sounds and speech patterns, say small words, and recognize familiar patterns in books and their immediate environments.

They have achieved a much larger degree of self-awareness, and the awareness of others. Their sense of object permanence is not yet fully developed, which is one reason that babies tend to cry when their parents so much as leave the room: they are not certain they will return.

Ten to twelve-month-old babies tend to communicate in more sophisticated ways, waving goodbye, and clinging to their parents whenever they feel threatened. Ten to twelve-month-old babies can move around to a certain extent, although usually not unaided by their parents, or at least pieces of furniture. They can bring finger foods to their mouths, drink liquids from sipping cups, turn pages in books, and play with balls.

By fifteen months, babies can walk unaided, squat, stand, and sit. They can climb stairs if they are aided by the railing. Babies a year old and older can start feeding themselves, playing with crayons, and start playing with construction toys and jigsaw puzzles. Babies are no longer quite as physically dependent on their parents, and are much freer to explore the world around them with their endless curiosity. Parents will have to keep a closer eye on them as a result, but not so much that their babies cannot explore. One-year-old babies develop larger vocabularies, expanding from under ten to about one hundred between the ages of one and two years old. They become unfortunately accustomed to using negation phrases, and making learned animal sounds.

One to two-year-old babies can recognize their own reflections as their selves, start with their pretend play, communicate, start to understand the nature of cause and effect, and understand more directives from their parents. Between fourteen to eighteen months, their pattern recognition skills have improved tremendously, as has their recognition of facial expressions. Babies can even start identifying different parts of their own bodies, as they get closer to two years of age. Babies' physical development increases very rapidly over the course of just their first years, and they have all but transformed in time for their second and third years of life.

Toddler (2 to 3 years old)

By age two, children often have vocabularies of between two hundred and three hundred words. They understand many basic concepts, including possession. Two-year-olds can know their own ages, names, and genders. They can start counting, and their problem-solving ability increases with practice. Their speech patterns are limited, but they can string simple sentences together well enough to communicate simple thoughts and desires. Toddlers can identify pictures, and some of their own body parts. They are starting to get a sense of self, and gain some level of autonomy, away from their parents.

Toddlers are famously negative, partly due to their developing understanding of others needs and boundaries. As such, toddlers have a tendency to fail to recognize other children as other people, and they have to be taught the concept of sharing. They are more likely to play beside other children than actively engaging with them. Toddlers are well known for being prone to emotional outbursts as they start learning how to regulate their own behavior patterns.

Toddlers are now adept at running and walking, can partially balance on one foot, and have even started to climb. They can ride tricycles, use straws, use doorknobs and lids, and play a much rider range of games. Their physical and mental development has been significant since only one-year prior. Parents can encourage their toddlers' emotional development further in many ways. Taking toddlers on trips outside the home, giving them more of a role in simple tasks around the house, if possible, and letting them begin trying to wash their own hands with and without your help, and put on and take off their own clothes, can all help them proceed in the right direction. Parents can play counting games with them, look at family photo albums together, play with cutouts and shapes, read rhymes, sing songs, and play games like 'Simon says' to encourage speaking and listening skills. Toddlers can play more than ever before and there are new opportunities to interact with them on new levels. They should take as many opportunities as possible to encourage their toddlers to play and explore the world, even giving them bath toys and cups. Ideally, they should keep tabs on how much television their toddlers watch, since interactive play activities are much more likely to encourage positive child development than passive activities like television, even if it is educational television.

Toddlers can seem uncooperative, but they want careful, loving attention as much as all other children, and they can still calm down enough for bonding. As toddlers turn three years old and approach preschool age, they can run, jump, and use staircases more easily than ever before, operate utensils unassisted, and a multitude of other tasks that require fine motor skills. Most of them should be toilet trained between two and three years old, and develop the bowel control to do so around that age.

Their attention spans improve, allowing them to finish things they start more easily. As children turn three, their language skills improve tremendously. They often have vocabularies of up to one thousand words; they can memorize catchy phrases, recognize colors, string together sentences of around four or five words, use simple greetings and gestures of politeness, and use their own names in conversations. Communicating with them is much easier than ever before, particularly since their own speech is much more comprehensible to others. Three-year-old children tend to be extremely inquisitive about the world, and for children, this tends to be when they go through their characteristic early 'why' phases. Three-year-olds calm down significantly from their 'terrible twos.' They can interact

More easily with others, lacking the emotional highs of a two-year-old. They moderate their feelings far more, and are capable of respecting other people's boundaries. Stimulating their burgeoning social skills and problem-solving abilities is of utmost importance at this age, to prepare them for school in a year or so. Ideally, they should interact with children of their own ages, with similar levels of social skills. Parents should try to promote socializing between their three-year-old children and others. They should try to get their children to be more active in conversation, perhaps get their children to tell stories to them, etc. Showing as much visible support as possible when three-year-old children practice their verbal skills is a great way to encourage them, and kids thrive on positive feedback from their parents at that age.

Fun activities for parents and three-year-olds include nursery rhymes and storytelling, puzzles, construction toys, playing 'dress-up,' art projects, and games like 'hide and seek.' Parents can take many opportunities throughout the day to help their children learn how to do certain things, and giving them as much encouragement as possible when they do them. Essentially, parents take a more interactive role in their children's creative and intellectual development as their children approach preschool and start to do so under the tutelage of other teachers.

Preschool-aged (4 to 5 years old)

Preschool-aged children improve in their physical and mental abilities even more. They can sing, build things, use staircases unassisted, start using simple tools like safety scissors, and learn their letters. Children can learn to tie their shoes at the preschool level, and dress and undress themselves more easily. They expand the number of words they can use per sentence, relate events, respond to instructions, and start talking more often. Preschool-aged children indulge in a lot of fantasy role-playing, but they are capable of discerning fantasy and reality. The fantasy role-play is pretend.

They also tend to want to learn more about the real world, which parents should only encourage. Preschool-aged children will start identifying names of things, and learning how to tell time, and recognize patterns in day-to-day life. Five-year-olds tend to be more sociable and agreeable than four-year-olds, and get into fights less often. They start to want to make other people around them happy, as they outgrow the more seemingly narcissistic behavior of very young children. They develop fears about the unexplored world, and may become attached to those around them, and try to work through those fears through play and fantasy. Parents should try to teach their children about the best ways to express emotions, and encourage their vast curiosity about the world.

School-aged (6 to 12 years old)

Children learn a wide range of social and a cademic skills when they are at school age. Around age six, children start losing their deciduous teeth, and growing their set of adult teeth. They keep busy with a wide range of activities, and starting forming their first peer groups over the course of their school years. Kids start associating with opposite-gender kids more often around the ages of eight and nine. As they get closer to twelve years old, they develop formal reasoning skills and the ability to think on a more abstract and philosophical level.

Parents should set aside time to spend with their school children each day. They should be sure to set good examples for them, since positive images of adults are especially crucial at this age. Parents can promote both physical activity and intellectual pursuits for their children. They should try to get them interested in different hobbies and activities with other kids to develop creative and social skills.

Adolescent (13-18 years old)

Adolescents start to think about the future far more, and plan ahead for adulthood. Teenagers may start caring more about global and societal concerned, and get involved in activism in junior high and high school, which parents should support and encourage. They have completed a life stage, namely childhood, and their sights are set forward. Teenagers are trying to find their place in the world and searching for their identities. It is normal for them to constantly wonder if what they are thinking and feeling is normal, appropriately enough. They may become much attached to what members of their peer groups say, and play more stocks in them than parental opinions as they try to establish some degree of independence.

Teenagers will face many new challenges, as they start to go through puberty. They may face problems with body image and peer pressure like never before. Parents may feel concerned about what their teenage children are getting up to, and it is important to start allowing adolescents some measure of independence no matter how concerned parents feel. The important thing is for parents to create a safe environment where teenagers feel they can talk to them. Parents who suspect their children may have mental health concerns should get them into therapy, but otherwise, giving teenagers space is still important to their development.

Being aware of what is going on in your teenager's lives is important for both of you, but being overly strict will just send them into hiding. Children may become that much more unwilling to talk to their parent as they approach adolescents, and parents should be careful not to force the issue too much.

Other times, they may be talking to parents while subtly reaching out for help. Parents should at least try to provide their teenagers with some safe places where they can communicate with adults, even adults other than their own parents if necessary. There are more resources than ever for struggling adolescents, and parents should encourage their children to look into them. They need to be made aware of the fact that adolescence, with all of its complex peer relationships, is also just a phase. Their lives will change as they emerge into adulthood.

Chapter 9: Family Time

You really need to be on the same page as your partner at all times. Talk about your work responsibilities away from the kids. This isn't their worry. Don't make the kids feel like they are nuisances in your life by reminding them all the time about your obligations. You need to decide between you and your partner:

Who will take the kids to school?

Which parent will represent the child at a school meeting?

Who will pick them up?

Is it possible for both parents to go to the school play?

Who is going to do the shopping this week?

You can save yourself a lot of time if you have one shopping day a week instead of dropping into the store every time you discover that you forgot something. Thus get the kids involved in writing things down when they use the last of something so you always have a good idea of what to buy. In order to improve the amount of family time that you have, arrange with your partner, one night a week that he stays with the kids while you do the shopping. There is nothing worse than shopping with kids because they will distract you and will also be making demands for things you would not normally buy. If you want to have a family outing for shopping that's different but for your groceries, try to do the shop in one hit. You can also use Internet delivery services, but they can be a bit of a pain because you have to be there to take the delivery.

Apart from the time that you want to spend with your family, the kids are going to have different things that they want to attend and it is encouraged that these are brought up at the evening meal and written down straight away so that there's no arguments about them. Similarly, if one parent is away from home, the other needs to compensate for the missing parent and if you know when those dates are likely to be, you can plan around them and make sure that you book in Skype calls so that the kids know daddy or mommy loves them and misses them.

It's a good idea to do things with the kids that involve a bit of exercise. Biking together or going to the woods or the beach are all family events that you can enjoy together. Because you work and life is pretty stressed out, you need this time to just chill out and enjoy your kids. Thus, try to avoid taking work home with you. You need to draw the line. Just as your boss doesn't expect your family life to intrude into your work life, you need to understand that your work life should not interfere with your family life. Let your boss know that you are not approachable at weekends and this frees you up to enjoy yourself with your family.

I suggest that if you have kids that are a little lazy, getting a pet is probably one of the best things you can do, but make it a manageable pet. A smaller breed of dog that is not snappy is the best bet because you can train the dog together and you can also make the child understand the responsibility of pet ownership and walking the dog. This novelty will drop off after a while, but if you reinforce the enjoyment of having a dog at regular intervals, the children should keep up their enthusiasm.

If you are finding that the kids are always at home with mom while dad is out enjoying himself, don't take it out on the kids. Talking to your partner is essential. These are his kids too and he needs to respect that family time means for all of the family and doesn't exclude him just because he thinks he is entitled to do what he wants. The best way around this is to have your own individual interests and make sure you allow for each other's absences. Perhaps he wants to go out and play cards with his buddies once a week, but if this is the case, remember parenting is a shared thing. Make sure you have something you want to do as well, so that no resentment comes into the picture.

As we said before, family time together doesn't have to involve expensive trips. It can mean doing artwork with the kids or helping them to build a fort in the garden. Whatever fits in with your family life are things that are valuable. Build a bird house and take it in turns to feed the birds. Teach your kids to enjoy the environment. Give them a small patch in the back yard to grow things and encourage them. Kids do enjoy this kind of thing but you have to understand that they may not be as fastidious at the tasks as a professional gardener. Encourage them from an early age by growing carrot tops in saucers because the delight that children experience with simple things like this makes up for all the time you spend away from the kids. They will remember all of these things that helped to shape their lives.

Chapter 10: Reasons For Suicide

Suicide is a horrible thing for parents to deal with. Many teenagers feel like it is the only way to get out of the sadness or other issues they are going through, but this just leaves behind a lot of people who are now sad and lost without the person they loved. While there are a lot of other ways out of the situation other than death, the person who is contemplating suicide is going to see this as the only way.

This is why it is so important to recognize when there are issues with your teenager and address these problems as soon as possible. Suicide is a permanent solution, one that can never be reversed, and acting with caution early on, and getting help even before the problem gets very bad can help to prevent this horrible ending. But first, you need to be able to recognize some of the warning signs that suicide may be an option that your teenager is considering.

Common Signs

Some of the common signs that you should look for in your teenager when it comes to suicide include:

Having hostile and aggressive behavior

Withdrawing from family and friends like they don't want to be around others anymore

Giving away important items to those they love

Having a preoccupation with death either in drawings, writing, and conversations

Making statements that are suicidal in nature

More risks being taken than before

A huge change in their personality, such as going from being an upbeat person to becoming someone who is quiet and withdrawn.

You should take all threats of suicide like they are serious. You may at first feel that they are made in jest, but you are missing out on helping out someone who is in need of help. Usually these are signs that something is wrong and you should get them the help that they need as soon as possible.

Things That Increase Suicidal Thoughts

There are a number of things that could increase the likelihood that your teen is going to have thoughts about suicide. These include:

A past history of being bullied

A past history of sexual abuse

An abusive or disruptive family life

Someone close to the teen, such as a hero, family member, or friend, who committed or attempted suicide

Attempted to commit suicide in the past

A parent with substance abuse or depression problems

Depression or some other mental health issue in the individual

If your teen has gone through some issues as school or in their home life recently, or they are dealing with depression in their daily life, you really need to be careful about them thinking over suicide. These issue could make the teen feel like things are helpless and they may start to look for things that are going to help them to feel better. Taking the time to be there for your teenager and getting them the help that is needed when they are sad, having trouble in school, or had a significant personal issue come up in life can help to prevent the permanent solution of suicide.

Chapter 11: The Six Steps Of Discipline

The good news is that most of the time when a child needs discipline, the events unfold in a reliable order for both you and your child. In this chapter I will go over what steps you need to take when your child experiences a behavior issue, as well as help you decide how to handle the situation no matter what it is your child has done.

I remember coming home from the grocery store one day; as I was putting away the groceries I noticed that my child was chewing gum. Knowing that I did not buy gum nor allow my children to chew it, I asked her where it came from. She told me a long story, and of course now I don't remember the details, but she had claimed that one of her brothers had given her the gum. After asking both of her brothers and finding that they had no idea what she was talking about, I asked her again. I knew at this point she had not only lied to me, but had most likely stolen the gum from the check-out at the store.

Of course, most of us can tell when our toddlers lie – they are not good at it and have not had enough practice to hide their lies. The problem is that many of us do not know how to respond to such a situation. Had her teenage brother stolen something from the store, I would have made him take it back to return it, confess, and pay for it if he had used it. This does not work too well with a toddler, and oftentimes brings more embarrassment onto the parent than the child. Therefore, many of these types of situations are not handled correctly.

The Six Steps:

☐ Your child displays a behavioral problem, does not follow the rules, or does something you disapprove of.

☐ Discovery – there are several ways that you could discover that your child has done something wrong, and different ways to react as well.

A.The child confesses to you. If the child confesses that he or she has done something wrong, then you know that your child does know right from wrong. What the child needs to learn at this point is how to control his impulses. These impulses could be due to any number of emotions, including anger, greed, or even simply laziness. The child also needs to understand that there are consequences for his behavior even when he knows that he has done wrong. Just because a child confesses does not mean that he is off the hook.

B.If you catch the child in the act, you have to know how to handle this as well. The first thing you want to think about is why you caught the child. Did the child want to be caught? It this some cry for attention? Did the child lack control of his emotions so badly that he lost control of his actions? The discipline that you will use will depend on why the child displayed the behavior and why the child was caught. You also will need to know this when you talk to your child after he has been disciplined.

C.If you have found that the child has tried to hide his behavior you need to know why he has done this as well. You need to figure out if the child hid his behavior because he was aware of the consequences and was afraid of them. Is the child afraid of you or what you will do if you find out that he or she has misbehaved? Is the child afraid of your disapproval? Is the child afraid of his or her own feelings of guilt? Did the child try to hide the behavior because he or she thought that they could get away with it?

☐☐Once you discover the behavior issue, the next step is to confront the child about the issue. This is where you will begin making decisions; you may need to take some time for yourself to determine what you are going to do. If your emotions are high and you are upset with your child, you will want to take a few minutes to think about what needs to be done.

If you are angry with your child or shocked by his behavior, it may be that your child will fear you while you are speaking instead of hearing what you are saying. No parent wants their child to be afraid of them; this is one reason why you need to take a step back and think about what needs to be done. Most of the time this will be done with older children, but if your toddler behaves very badly you may need to take a break before determining what you will do.

This is the time that you need to decide if you will comfort your child before handing down discipline. There will be times when your child is afraid of his own behavior and if you try to discipline without helping the child calm down, oftentimes he will simply tell you that he did not do it.

Let's take an example – if your child steals a toy, instead of jumping down the child's throat with How could you do this?-type questions, it is best to ask calm questions such as, "Would you like to explain to me what happened?" or "Is this what you want me to believe?" or even "Are you sure that is what happened?".

These questions should be asked until the child confesses to the behavior. If you know that your child will lie about his or her behavior before you ask the question, say something like "We both know that this toy does not belong to you, and it can be hard to face what you have done, but let's talk about it."

Most of the time when confrontation happens, it involves yelling and fighting, and people end up with their feelings hurt. Instead, when you confront your child about his behavior, remain calm and use a soothing voice. Let the child know that he or she can trust you and that he or she is not bad just because they chose to display bad behaviors.

⛶ After confrontation comes acknowledgment. The child may at this point continue to deny his behavior in an attempt to lie his way out of the discipline that he knows will take place. He may also fear admitting that he behaved badly, because he feels guilty about the way that he behaved. This is the time that you will help your child work through his feelings about what he has done. Explain to the child that brave people admit when they have done something wrong, and that the discipline is not to hurt him or her, but to remind the child not to behave that way in the future.

Once the child understands why he is being punished and admits what he has done, it is time to deal with the consequences and it is time for the child to make amends. The goal of discipline is for your child to understand that there are consequences for his behavior and to think about these consequences before he behaves in the same way again.

The child needs to care about himself or herself enough to not want to face the consequence again and to think about their own behavior. The best consequences and most effective ones are the ones that are tied to the behavior. One example of this might be if the child were to steal a toy from a friend – the child would have to take the toy back and apologize. You could also take away one of the child's favorite toys so that he understands what it is like to lose something that he cares about.

The consequences need to be fair and they need to teach a lesson. If the consequences are not fair or do not teach a lesson, the child will be left feeling upset, angry with you, and confused. There will be no lesson learned and the behavior will persist.

⬜Forgiveness is the final step. Your child will not learn from bad behavior unless he understands that he can be forgiven for what he has done, that there is a potential for good behavior, and that he does not have to face discipline when he behaves well. After the child has faced the consequences, talk to the child. Let the child know that you still love him, give him a hug, and tell him that you forgive him but expect him to think about that behavior next time.

Discipline does not have to be difficult, and if you follow these steps it can be very easy. Each time you need to discipline your child, walk through these steps to make sure that none are skipped. This will ensure that your child learns from his behavior and does not repeat it in the future.

These steps can be used for any behavior and can be used even on children that have been diagnosed with behavior problems. The one thing you have to do in order for these steps to work is to ensure that you are being consistent.

Chapter 12: The Good And The Not-So-Good Parent

When children eat sweets, cakes and all the other "weird" stuff before breakfast one cannot help but question the authority behind them. When they seem to have a carte-blanche on TV programs especially those of obscene content, one cannot help but wonder whose children are they. Most subjects have two extremes on either end, parenting is no different. Doing things within reason is subject to abuse, rejection and perhaps, in some cases, ridicule.

Some of us have experienced, witnessed and even heard most bizarre things that relate to parenting. I know a boy whose uncle once beat him with a stick so bad he had bumps all over his head and also rendered his right arm useless for days, he had trouble sleeping because of the injuries he sustained. The reason for such a beating was a missing pigs head, the uncle had cooked the pork for the family and it went missing only to discover on the following morning that the family cat was indulging himself under the bed with his most coveted catch. The uncle administered the punishment during his drunken state, the way he enjoyed himself you would bet he was winning at his favourite sport. This man was still dealing with the reality of his wife leaving him for good. I also witnessed a sober woman throw a red-hot poker to the thigh of a twelve-year-old girl one afternoon, after a wonderful school day, while building a coal-fire in the Defy stove using a poker to move the coals around in the stove. The argument ensued between her and a twelve-year-old girl, in an instant the red-hot rod was stuck on the little girl's thigh and she ran, screaming all the way to the next-door neighbour's house with the poker still smoking on her thigh. An old woman helped to remove the rod with great shock. The woman who threw the poker on the little girl's thigh was a married woman whose husband did not spend more than two months at home with his family each year; she was practically single. This is the same woman who tied her own daughter to the foot of the bed wrists and ankles and gave her one of the fiercest beatings I have ever witnessed and this happened in the full view of us all who were in that house that merciless night. I was only ten years old at the time.

One afternoon after a long day's work, workers were queuing for the lift in the block of flats where I was residing when I heard a woman tell a tale like story of "giving my son all he wants" and she did so with the smile of contentment. The little fellow was a three year old brat who was said to be used to having his way in the shops whenever he went with his mother. The content mother was proud of "spoiling my son" to quote her exact words. The friend to whom the story was related to was left speechless and so were the rest of us who were listening to their conversation. The storyteller was a single mother of two.

Character flaws of us all sometimes depicts a rather blur pictograph of our imperfect pasts. We are the products of those who have, I say HAVE, an upper hand over our lives, those who influence our decisions even after they are long gone from this earth.

Children who get to have their way from birth till adulthood are often envied by those whose plight is their parent(s)' (or guardian) revenge against all who ever ill-treated them when they were young and yet this so called revenge is now directed at another helpless victim.

The fact that God gives out guidelines, I mean ONLY guidelines on how we should raise our young ones is proof enough of how much confidence He has on the work of His hands. He has confidence in us so much that He does NOT impose "24-laws you must know before you become a parent"; "17-fomulae of perfect child rearing". The freewill He has, the same He withheld not, so that we can by choice either build or break our children.

If God by some chance upheld a notion that a fear driven conformity to His principles could result in perfect human race, He could NOT have given us a free will so strong no external power or influence can successfully manipulate without our choice of yielding to it. A story is told of a toddler who was running riot in the isles of a church while his father was preaching. The preacher reprimanded the little brat to no avail. He finally left the pulpit, got him by the scruff of his neck and literally pinned him on a chair in the congregation's full view. The little brat exclaimed to everyone's amazement, "Out I'm sitting but inside I'm standing".

Learning to keep perfect balance between two extreme parenting practices is good enough by any human standard. What is socially acceptable is often advocated and defended by each society as though it were a Gospel Truth. Anyone who isolates himself from accepted social behaviour and principles of life is digging himself a bottomless pit so he can drag his family along with him into destruction. A very solid family and or social support system is necessary to all who aspire to raise children whether married or single. One's kinfolks especially, play an undeniably vital role in adding value to a child. When you lay down certain basic principles with your kinfolk regarding things like discipline and submitting to the authority of "elders", then half the work is done in the light of your village raising your child.

This support system is indispensable in that it is the necessary additional role modelling for your child/-ren. It is the responsibility of all parents to foster a healthy relationship between his child and his relatives especially while all is going well. You should be able to discuss with your relatives things like who to entrust your child to in the event that you are hospitalised for a lengthy period or in some worst cases when death strikes. Parenting demands that we should all take care of these things while our feet still tap to our favourite music. No one can dispute the fact that children who have healthy normal relationships with their relatives when all is well, are well poised to adjust and adapt far better than those who did not even know about their relatives in the event that their parent/s are no longer available to care for them. We daily face challenges like permanent disability, mental incapacitating illnesses (like falling into deep long coma), kidnapping, imprisonment and death. One's child and relatives ought to know what to do under these circumstances in the event that they happen. Being a single parent does not mean that the child is yours alone!

Chapter 13: 10 Quick Tips To Deal With Toddler Tantrums

Tantrums are a part of almost every child's toddler stage. Although temper tantrums are common, many parents do not know how to control or tame them. A tantrum can be a bad habit that needs to be corrected, or it could be an indicator that the child has a need that hasn't been met. Whether a tantrum happens at home, in a friend's home, a formal setting or in a public place, it can be difficult to deal with if the parents are not prepared. Here are ten different methods to implement when a toddler throws a tantrum.

Acknowledge Their Feelings

The first thing every parent should do when a tantrum begins is to find out why the child is behaving erratically in the first place. Sometimes there could be an underlying problem. For example, if the toddler throws tantrums during evening meals, the issue could be that it isn't the right time to serve a meal and mealtime should be pushed back to a later hour. Some parents let their children participate in the preparation of their meal. This often prevents tantrums from happening because the child feels involved in the process.

Sleep time or day nap time is another common situation in which temper tantrums occur; most of the time it is because the child is overtired and can't seem to calm down for rest, or if it is during the day, it may be the wrong time to try to put the toddler to sleep. Documenting when tantrums take place will help parents figure out what exactly triggers it. If it is a legit problem that can be solved, then it should be solved in the most reasonable way without time out.

Change the Setting

If you are in a public place, a sudden tantrum can be an embarrassing situation. Taking your toddler to a quieter place or even leaving the area can change the course of everything. Once the child has calmed down, it is the right time to let the child know that throwing fits and making a scene is wrong. Since children sometimes use temper tantrums to manipulate a situation to go their way, they will eventually understand that throwing fits is not the right way to gain an adult's attention if the adult responds by changing the setting.

Ignore the Theatrics

If a child is having a fit in a private place like in the home or a friend's home and the fit is simply an attempt to get their way, it is wise to ignore it and remain within the child's sight. This will let them now that the fit won't work. If you do not acknowledge the tantrum, there is no reason for the child to use it again after realizing there are no results. Another way to ignore a tantrum is to distract the child by giving other options such as coloring or eating something. If the child is easily distracted from a tantrum it may be an indicator that the fit was not caused by anything serious.

Give the Toddler Time Out

Time out is a popular consequence of bad behavior in toddlers. It is effective because it gives them time to think about what they did. It also serves as a warning that time out may be given to them again if they take the same wrong action in the future. If your toddler threw a fit as a result of being told to share a toy or another action that would have created good habits, time out is a good method to use as a solution.

Remind Them of the Consequences

It is always good to remind the child of the consequences of their tantrums if you have already used the time out method. Whether you are in a public place or at home, your toddler should develop a respect for you that reinforces good behavior.

Keep Calm

Never neglect yourself when it comes to dealing with your child's tantrums. You should always take deep breaths and go outside when these things happen. Dealing with theatrical fits can be disheartening. Make sure you are in your right mind at all times, before and after the fit. If you ever feel like you can't deal with your toddler or that you might lose your own temper and say hurtful things, make sure you have another adult available to watch over your toddler while you take a break and get some fresh air.

Plan Ahead of Time

Planning on what solutions you will implement for each type of situation according to setting is important. You will be less worried and nervous about whether your child will throw a tantrum if you know that you are already prepared for it. Writing down the different places you take your toddler and putting the solutions next to each setting in a chart will help you remember and solidify your techniques.

Reason With Your Child

Communication is the most important thing when it comes to raising children. If there is a line of communication between you and your toddler, there will be fewer tantrums. If you reason with your child by asking what is wrong or stating that certain behaviors are wrong, you are opening up communication even if the child does not understand everything you are saying. Once you start to speak to your toddler like you are speaking to someone your own age your child will feel important regardless of how difficult your words may be to understand. Your child will also respond to your tone, which will most likely be calm if you are in reasoning mode.

Comfort Your Child

It is good to embrace your toddler a few hours after the fit. This helps the child realize that love and discipline can co-exist and that discipline does not indicate an absence of love.

Make Eye Contact with Your Toddler

You must always make eye contact with your child after tantrums. Let your toddler know that hitting and other things done during tantrums are wrong. Eye contact will reinforce everything you say, and toddlers who do not speak full sentences can still understand if you are pointing out bad behavior.

All of the methods above should be implemented according to the setting and cause for the fit. These methods will make it easier for parents to deal with tantrums or avoid them effectively.

Chapter 14: How To Get Your Child To Talk About Their Feelings

It hurts when you can't get your child to open up to you, no matter how hard you try. If that's your situation right now, here are some ways to encourage your child to talk about their feelings:

• Ask fun and engaging questions. If you are the type of parent that asks questions like "How was school today?" I bet you got a short response such as "Fine" or "Alright". Some children won't elaborate unless you ask the right questions. Open-ended questions like "Did you do anything today that you are proud of?", "You're in a cheerful mood, what did I miss?", "Why is rugby your favourite sport and not tennis?" etc. are more likely to draw out the lengthened response that you are after.

• Create a connect. Sometimes, your child fails to tell you anything because there is a disconnect between the two of you. To overcome this, create an atmosphere that allows your child to feel safe and supported. That way, they will come to you with their little problems and big problems, knowing full well that they have your support and understanding, no matter what. When you can create an open and honest connection with your child, they will be more open to telling you things, even without you having to prompt.

•Give your child space. There are times when children just want to be left alone. When you sense that, give your child the privacy and respect to try and process their emotions by themselves.

How Beliefs and Thoughts Arise in Children

Two children can have the same experience, yet have two very different reactions. For example; Bella and Remy both get invited to a birthday party from a classmate, Bella's thoughts/beliefs are "Yes! Yummy party food", "I love party games", "It's a good chance to play with my friends". These thoughts lead to Bella feeling happy and excited. On the other hand, Remy's thoughts/beliefs are "I bet I will be left out of the party games", "No one will play with me" "I will be embarrassed in front of my classmates". These thoughts lead Remy feeling worried and anxious. Children's beliefs are the expectations of what they think is most likely to occur in that situation. Think of beliefs like wearing a pair of glasses. We all have a different pair and therefore see the world differently, due to our past experiences. At such a young age, belief systems in children develop mainly through social modelling and the messages that they receive from their surrounding environment. For most children, this will be in the home from parents, siblings and grandparents. And at school by their peers and teachers.

Keeping a Thought Diary

Keeping a thought diary can help your child to combat worries and anxiety. Each child has thoughts in their mind which can be undetectable by us parents. By encouraging your child to write down their thoughts and feelings, you will have talking points so that you can help challenge their unhelpful thinking habits. As such, whenever your child has an unpleasant feeling you should encourage them to write it down under the following headings, in four columns:

•Situation. Writing down the exact moment in which they feel worried or anxious. Children who are afraid and anxious tend to avoid certain situations. Writing them down will enable you to pinpoint precisely what these scenarios are and how best to move forward. Example; I got picked last for the sports team.

•Thoughts. Help your child to put their negative thoughts in writing. It will enable them to process it better and allow you to gain insight into their reasoning. Encourage your child to write down any negative thoughts associated with each situation. This will allow you to know how best to help them challenge their negative thinking habits. Example; No one likes me.

• Feelings. Assist your child to write down how the specific situation and thought made them feel. Example; Sad.

• Helpful thought. (See chapter five for details).

Chapter 15: Positive Discipline With Clear Expectations Instill Good Behavior

There are times when our kids try our patience by knowing exactly how to push our buttons. With that said it's easy to feel many different emotions as a result of feeling angry or annoyed. Although being a good parent is really put to the test when this happens it is extremely important to show kindness yet stay firm when it comes to doing the necessary discipline. We need to remove any thoughts of physical or verbal abuse and replace it with positive discipline with clear expectations. They will learn that these things are wrong and at the same time know that getting yelled at or being hit isn't part of your positive discipline techniques.

The goal of positive discipline is to teach our kids to be responsible by being cooperative, showing kindness, and respect for others. Consistency is by far the easiest way to teach them this. Linking the same punishment to the same misconduct and discussing their discipline openly and with complete honesty.

There are other things besides age to keep in mind when deciding what form of discipline you are intending to use for your child. Their maturity level and temperament should also be considered before implementing any action. You need to have a detailed discussion with them so they understand in advance what to expect. This will allowthem to learn from their misbehavior so they can avoid having the same actions in the future. Remember to let them know it is not them you dislike it is their chosen behavior you do not approve of.

A good parent will take time to reflect on what their child has done before responding with any immediate discipline. It will allow you to control any anger you feel and not go overboard with too harsh of action that isn't warranted.

A good parent keeps an open mind and is always learning from their kids. Every child is unique so we must realize that there are different forms of discipline and not all forms of discipline work. Everyone makes mistakes so we must consider and adjust the discipline to fit each individual child. We must strive to have a positive outcome by showing some understanding and love.

Clear expectations instill good behavior but there are times when it is very difficult to communicate anything with our kids. A good parent works hard to establish what types of behavior are acceptable and at the same time clarify right from wrong. Make sure there is consistency in what rules are to be followed for all situations which will eliminate any confusion for you the parent and your child.

Sitting down with your kids well ahead of time to outline what is expected of them and the consequences for not adhering to your guidelines is a must do for good parents. They need to understand that there is no room to negotiate at the time they misbehave and that you will be firm in your discipline. Let them know that when it comes to their safety or welfare that you alone are responsible to decide what is best for them. Be sure that all discussions are open and honest so the end result is having everyone on the same page.

If need be draft a contract between you and your kids. Keep it simple and easy to understand. Developing a different format like a good behavior chart might work better for younger kids. There could also be weekly awards earned when there are no violations of the contract. This will connect their good behavior with being able to do something special they really enjoy. Don't be too surprised if that turns out to be more fun time with Mom or Dad. What all kids need to understand is the positive discipline they receive from you is a method of teaching them what is acceptable behavior. Although your kids will have the tendency to not adhere to your rules or guidelines, down deep they also know it is what is best for them in the long run. It allows them to grow as individuals and start making smart decisions on their own. Positive discipline with clear expectations can do nothing but instill good behavior.

Chapter 16: Help Them Have Confidence

Parents' only way of gaining the trust and winning back the confidence of their children is to build their children's self-confidence. Children who are difficult to handle often have low moral and self-confidence.One of the reasons why children could be rebellious is that their confidence is beyond low level and their parents never know about it.Parents usually are so proud of their children and expect too much from them.Such expectations could always drive their children to insanity especially if they are not what their parents think they are.This could result to a more difficult situation and to some children, this could lead to behaving unlikely so that their parents will no longer expect too much from them.

The issues of how to restore children's confidence could really be one of the major problems that parents are facing.This parenting problems could go from one generation to the next and still it remains a problem to most people. This could not be resolved overnight either, but it definitely needs constant monitoring and constant practice to gain consolable results. The following suggestions could at least help parents in winning back their children's confidence in order to become regular persons once more.

Motivation

Motivation could always help a person do the things that he wants in his own way. Parents who often motivate their children could always have successful children. Children with low confidence, troubled children, or difficult to handle children may lack some parental motivation. Parents are known to be the children's strong fortress and without their support children could go astray. This could happen especially if both parents are so busy with their own lives, with their businesses, or with their professions and their children usually suffer the consequences.

Parents should see to it that they have a well-balanced life so that they could help their children's growth as well.A motivation that is well-planned is not mainly coaching their children to do well; parents should always be guiding and coaching their children at the same time.One best motivation of parents could be through boosting the confidence of their children through praising their little success and supporting their failures.

Parental presence

Material things could be nothing to children if their parents cannot be with them most of the time.It is usually the mistake of parents to think that they need to work hard for their children.Material things may not matter to their children, as long as they are around when they need them; it would all that their children could ask for.It has been known that most children who have been very difficult to handle are those children of the very busy parents.Practically, their being difficult could always be their way of getting their parents' attention as well as their presence.Parents should always see to it that they will have time for their children to physically be with them especially during school activities and special occasions.If only parents could make themselves available for their kids most of the time, coaxing and coaching them, their children's confidence in them will surely return.

Spend time together regularly

The children would love to be with their parents.The reason behind this could be purely psychological that they must always know that their family is intact and happy.Parents should always include on their schedule regular family bonding at least once a week, twice a month, or monthly.They should make sure that everyone in their family knows this regular schedule so that relationships among them could foster and promote stability.Bonding could be in the forms of dining out, playing, picnic at the beach, or even travel.This way, their children who may be difficult to handle could unwind themselves, relax and enjoy more being with them.

Chapter 17: Communication Basics For Parents

Learning how to change your communication patterns through divorce can be challenging, but it is undeniably in the best interests of your children. Many parents willingly indicate that they would be more than happy to change their communication style from one of conflict to one of collaboration - however the other parent will never change, so what can they really accomplish?

The answer in one word is EVERYTHING. Communication is a two-sided activity, so if one person changes their tone, message, body language or attitude, it will automatically have an effect on the other party. The great news is that there are several techniques that you can use to change your communication style to decrease conflict and improve the quality of your interactions with your co-parent, whether they are aware of the techniques or not. In addition, all these techniques can also be used with your children or in any other type of stressful or difficult conversation in your life.

REFRAMES

Reframes are a way of summarizing both the emotion as well as the content of the other person's message, plus adding on what you think they would like to see differently. This has a way of allowing the other person to feel validated, allowing them to understand that you get their point, and then moving the conversation through to a problem solving mode rather than getting stuck in the blame or "its your problem" mode.

The example below outlines how a reframe can be used:

Mom: I am sick and tired of always having to clean all the kids' clothes when they get home. Just because you never had to do the laundry when we were together doesn't mean that you don't have to do it now. I don't appreciate this pile of laundry to do every time you bring the kids back here.

Dad's Reframe: You feel frustrated that I bring the kids back with their laundry not done and it seems to you that you aren't appreciated. It also sounds like it would be better for you if I did the laundry at my house, is that right?

OR

Dad's Reframe (2): You feel stressed having to do all the kids laundry when I bring them home, seems like you don't feel appreciated. Sounds like this is a real problem for you I hadn't considered. If I did it at my house, would that help out?

Either option is likely to result in Mom and Dad solving this problem together, rather than resulting in an escalation about the laundry and Mom's stress at having to get it done.

Reframes are short, easy and relatively simple, but they do require that you are actively listening to the other person and trying to really hear what they are saying, not just looking at what the surface issue may be.

"I" MESSAGES

"I" messages are taught in most communication classes and even assertiveness trainings. They are really a more formulated response that includes some of the same elements of a reframe, just with more detail and specificity. "I" messages are great for more complex problems that need more information and possibly even more problem solving and collaborative skills.

The formula for and "I" message as it applies to something happening that is causing a problem or distressing the children follows this pattern:

I feel (an emotion word) when (something specific happens) since it affects the children by (give a specific example of impact on the kids). I would like to talk about (specific positive change in behavior), can we agree or discuss this further (when will it happen)?

A good example of when to use an "I" message might be if one parent is chronically late to pick up the kids. Instead of being hostile and ready to give the other parent a piece of your mind when they arrive at the door, how about calmly stating:

I feel frustrated when the kids aren't picked up on time since it affects the children by causing them to have to wait and worry that they might miss their chance to spend time with you. I would like to talk about what time will work best to be consistent with their pick-up; can we agree to discuss this by phone on Tuesday at 8:00 when the kids are in bed?

Using the formula gives you a chance to rehearse and practice the "I" message and prevents you blurting out a negative or hostile comment that is likely to cause the other parent to become defensive, resulting in the same old negative communication styles. Children overhearing this conversation will see

Mom and Dad problem solving through communication, not arguing and accomplishing nothing.

PARENTING ROLES VERSUS MARRIAGE ROLES

It is critical to separate the roles of an ex-husband and ex-wife from the roles as co-parents. Keep in mind that this is now a business relationship of raising your children in the most positive, calm and supportive environment possible for your kids. Whatever negative issues caused the divorce, they have to be put into the past and into perspective. The marriage roles as husband and wife are over and restructuring to be co-parents is going to take some adjustment. If you have a lot of negative thoughts and feelings towards the other parent, seek help and counseling for yourself. This will only help you be a better co-parent and help support your children through this restructuring process. Kids that see Mom and Dad being civil and respectful of each other will adjust to the divorce much more quickly than those that see ongoing hostility and anger.

Avoid asking personal questions, questions about finances that don't apply to the children or about new relationships if this is a sensitive area. If you do need to discuss a potentially hot button topic, do it when the children are not present or absolutely will not be able to overhear the conversation. Remember, even telephone conversations can be harmful for kids to overhear if parents are upset or angry.

Chapter 18: Every Second Matters

Raising your kids is not easy. But raising them to become good adults is even harder. Sometimes, your kids fail to appreciate or recognize your efforts but that comes with being a parent. You just have to be patient and love them.

Though there is no exact recipe for a perfect home and a set of guidelines that will turn you into the perfect parent, you can become a good parent to your kids. Providing for them financially is a good thing but being actually involved in your kids' life is even better.

Spend as much time as you can with them. Your kids won't stay young forever. Every second that you choose to spend at work or away from them is a second you'll never get back. Don't wait for the moment when you look at your kids and realize they're grown up but you don't really know anything about them.

Give them the attention they need and the love they deserve. As much as possible, don't let your work distance you from your kids. Let it be a factor that will drive you closer to them.

Whenever spending time with them, avoid checking your emails or checking your phone for updates regarding your work. Make that time about them and not about you or your job. You think you know your kids but you'll be surprised with the things you'll learn about them once you get to really spend time together.

Make it a point to always reflect on each other's actions. Have a heart to heart talk and go over your problems. Talk things through and plan activities together.

Your presence in your children's life affects them more than you think it does. It can help mold them into better persons or become the reason they feel detached and abandoned.

Parenting is not easy, but it is worth it. Just like money, the time spent with your kids matters so make the most of it.

Remember, like Zig Ziglar once said, "You never know when a moment and a few sincere words can have an impact on a life."

Chapter 19: Tips For Building Responsibility

How you view responsibility can affect the way you bring up your child to be responsible. If you see responsibility as a hard task, you will instill this idea in your child's mind making them afraid of taking up responsibilities. However, you need to understand that life is all about taking responsibilities from responsibility at your place of work, responsibility to your spouse, children, family, friends, society and the country meaning that there is no two way of about responsibilities; you cannot escape from teaching your child about responsibilities. Remember that you will not be with your children all the time especially when they grow up. Consequently, you ought to teach them how to take care of themselves. Below are some important tips that will help you bring up responsible children.

Give Out Responsibilities

You should never feel that giving your child responsibility is a form of punishment. Household chores should be divided among your children. While giving tasks, ensure that you give up age appropriate tasks. While a five year old may not wash the dishes, they can help you sort out laundry. It is important for a child to grow up knowing that work is meant to be for everyone and seeing their parents doing all the work does not mean that they are exempted from taking responsibility. Fulfilling those responsibilities you have assigned such as assisting with household chores gives your child a sense of achievement and confidence.

Don't Expect Much

You should always learn to manage your expectations as a parent when giving your child a chore to do. When the child has finished doing the household chores, be ready to congratulate them for the job well done even if they haven't done it the right way. You can say "I am so happy that you cleaned your room today". Praising your child makes them more confident since as we all know, kids are always looking for approval from their parents. Limiting your expectations will also help you to willingly assist your child where they fall short.

Create A Routine

Routines help in perfecting skills. You should make daily plans of what your child is supposed to do. In this case, have clear morning tasks like washing face, brushing teeth, making their bed, time for playing etc and late in the evening tasks like helping in clearing the table after dinner. When your child gets into the daily routine, they are able to pick up quickly on responsibilities. The routine will also make them get involved and in turn instill self-discipline. You can print the timetable and stick it in your child's room for them to remember. At the end of the day, it won't hurt you calling them and asking to be taken through what they did that day.

Enable Decision Making

Responsibility comes with lots of decision making, Present your child with choices during the course of daily activities. Giving your child decision-making power encourages independence. Examples of decisions a child can make include choice of clothing, snacks and play activities. When allowing them to make decisions, also teach them that every decision has a consequence, which they should accept whether good or bad. This is important, as your child needs to take responsibility of the decisions they make from young age so that they cannot be the kind of people who grow up to blame others for their misfortunes.

Lead The Way

If a certain task is to be done, make sure you do it in the way it is supposed to be done and show your child. Do not expect your son or daughter to do a chore that they are not familiar with and expect results. If it is mowing the grass, take a mower and ensure that your teenage boy or daughter can see what you are doing so that they know how to do it the next time even without your supervision.

Additionally, it is not advisable to choose work that you feel is a bore and give it to the child. Look for chores that are fun and involving to make the child view the task as positive. Responsibilities should not always be portrayed as tough to your child or else they will not be willing to undertake any responsibilities.

Create A Sense Of Independence

You need to start feeling comfortable while allowing your children some form of independence. As a parent, you will sometimes feel uncomfortable letting your child do things on their own because you somehow believe that they might end up being hurt. For example, if you are always afraid of letting your child to use the bus or even go shopping on his or her own, you might end up making the child fail to develop his or her independence. You should start by teaching your child how to scan his or her surroundings and take the right actions when he or she feels uncomfortable about the surroundings. Children learn from parents by observing so it is best to combine your verbal advice with the right actions to back up what you are saying. Additionally, teach your child self-care skills, such as taking a bath or shower on their own. Once they gain mastery of those basic skills, they have a foundation for trying more complex tasks. A child who learns how to serve themselves at home feels more comfortable serving themselves at a friend's house or even learning to prepare meals on their own.

Foster Accountability

A culture of accountability should be embedded in your home from the time your child is young. Without accountability in place, children tend to blame others for their actions, refuse to follow rules they find unfair, and find ways to justify their behavior. It is encouraged that children be responsible for their actions as that is the only way they will be able to have discipline. For example, if part of your son's daily routine is washing the dishes, you should not spare your child from doing so. You should call them, remind them what they were supposed to do and tell them to wash the dishes without delay. Accountability helps the child in knowing that there are consequences of doing some acts. This will thus enable them to work towards success, as they would want to bear positive fruits of their hard work. The bottom line is that no one in the family should get away with changing the rules to fit their needs or feelings.

Chapter 20: Pavlov's Dogs

What are the things you want to change about your way of thinking? Or doing? What patterns do you want to change? Write them down as they come into your head, then think about ways that you can retrain your mind.

Engage in Positive or Grateful Activities

The Internet is full of positivity and gratitude projects. On Instagram there are things like the Embrace Happy project, which also runs on Facebook. There are 100 Happy Days projects and 365Grateful. There are so many projects that you can take part in to try to force yourself to focus on the good things in life – not to suppress the bad, but to not be overwhelmed by it.

It's my experience that by spending just a few minutes a day writing down, photographing or otherwise recording the beautiful moments, we can look back and remember the good things, despite the bad.

I used to run a project called Mamatography. The idea was that mothers would take one photo every day that summed up their day, or that was special in their day. For three years I did this almost every day. I had a newborn baby, so some days were nothing days. I did nothing. I washed laundry. I cleaned up baby sick. I breastfed. That's all.

One of my favourite photos from those early new born days is a photo of baby boots all hung up on the washing line. It feels special, remembering the size of her feet.

Remembering those domestic bliss days – exhausting, frustrating, boring at times, but in retrospect, one of the happiest times of my life.

Find a happiness project that resonates with you, whether that's a writing project, or doodling, or photography or journaling, find it, stick to it and see the difference it makes in your life.

Activity 11: Engage in positive and thankfulness activities

Do a little research, and choose one or more projects to engage in. Choose something that fits with your interests, or come up with something entirely your own. Write down ones that you might be interested in as short term projects, or longer term projects that can become part of your every day life. Involve your children too, if appropriate, like a daily 'family gratitude' journal or similar.

Watch your Time Fillers

We've all been there.

It's been a busy day. The kids are finally in bed. You sink down in front of the telly, just to kill a little time, and before you know it, it's after midnight and you've filled your head with hours of rubbish TV.

That's an obvious time filler that can be avoided – and you'll probably feel better for avoiding it.

But there are others – the hours we spend on Facebook. The hours we spend mindlessly scrolling. There are so many other things you can do with that time.

I'm not saying close your Facebook account. I'm saying limit yourself. Don't lose days and weeks of your life, just because you don't want to think, and don't want to confront what's going on in your life.

I've been wanting to write this book for months. A few weeks ago I switched the TV off, put my old "studying" playlist of music on, and just began writing. By then end of the evening I had an outline in place, I knew what I wanted to say. And I got to watch 'my program' on catch-up the next day anyway.

Watch your time fillers, because they may take your mind off your loss, your divorce, the decisions you have to make for your future for a short while, but they will not help you sort through your problems, and they will not bring solutions.

Killing time adds to your overwhelm. Filling your head with Facebook, Instagram, Twitter, TV, chat rooms and similar takes time from things you could be doing to help yourself. You could be doing tomorrow's lunches, making your morning easier. You could be cutting the vegetables for dinner, making the "witching hour" easier.

That's not to say that you should never have down time – heaven knows we all need it. But not at the cost of your longer-term happiness.

By unpacking the dishwasher or dish rack while the kettle boils five times a day, I save myself 20 minutes in the evening – 20 minutes that I can much better use doing something I enjoy once the kids are asleep!

We can make all the excuses we want but we are the ones who suffer most.

I read an article about a woman who completed her high school diploma via her phone because she had no computer and no money for one. Hard? Yes! Does that take determination? Yes! Has it improved her job prospects? Has it improved her future options, her finances, her opportunities? Has it done wonders for her self esteem? Has it given her children something to look up to? Yes, yes, yes and yes! For someone going through a hard time it also serves as a distraction, but one with a positive end result.

Time fillers are another of those triggers. They become a habit. They dull our senses. They occupy our attention, and they rob us. And we'll only see it down the line, when we wonder where all the years have gone.

Chapter 21: Preparing Yourself

For effective positive discipline, a parent must be equipped with certain skills. This strategy certainly requires a parent to have a sense of self-control and self-awareness. Awareness enables a parent to see the connection between his own behaviors and responses to that of the child's. Remember, most undesirable behaviors in a child have an underlying reason. It is most often in response to the kind of attention, care and relationship they have with the parents. Self-control is also very important. It is inherently easier to yell than to lovingly reprimand a misbehaving child. Keep your emotions in check. In case you are too tired or stressed and is on the verge of losing your temper, walk away and calm yourself. Deal with the child afterwards. This will reduce the chances of an all-out yelling at the child.

Patience is a virtue. In this case, it is a must. You need to be patient in explaining to the child why the behavior is wrong, or what the consequences will. Change is a slow process in most kids. It may take some time before certain negative behaviors change or disappear. Parents also need to have a determined spirit in helping their children change undesirable behaviors. They must be willing to commit 100% of their time and efforts to be with their children and to understand them.

When parents deal with their children, they should have genuine interest and concern. They should also learn and understand the developmental stages that their children go through, and the factors that could affect them at these stages. Work on establishing an open, friendly, and genuine communication. Be your kids' closest friends while maintaining your authority as the parents.

Rewards are also an important aspect of positive discipline. Good behaviors should be appropriately praised and rewarded. Give attention to desirable behaviors, rather than negative ones. Rewards may be tangibles like toys. Keep it small and inexpensive. It may be mistaken as a bribe or that one needs to be good to receive gifts. Certain privileges can also be given or increased. More play time or giving permission to use certain items is a good way to acknowledge good behavior. Giving more responsibility is also a reward. It actually makes the child more independent, while reinforcing the good behavior. Example is letting the child care for his own things with less interference from the parents.

Chapter 22: Smart Kids Are Motivated

Motivation is about the fun of solving problems, and about perceiving the task at hand as being desirable, challenging, and worth the trouble of reaching that specific goal. It's also about creating interest and relevance.

A literal definition of motivation is the desire to do things. It's accompanied by an interest, or sense of enthusiasm and commitment to accomplish a task or goal. The motivation an individual has is usually on a continuum – I may be interested in photography as a hobby, but not interested (or motivated) enough to be a professional photographer.

This may also happen because I think I'll never be able to learn all the camera and lens options I should know, or simply because I'm more motivated to study biology. Motivation is a combination of many things – perceived difficulty or danger (which may result in a fear of failure), level of interest, having or not having a specific goal in mind, or lack of meaningful incentives.

THEORIES OF MOTIVATION

Theories are simply someone's way of describing things or actions that aren't easily visible. In astronomy, 'black holes' are described through mathematical formulas and theories about how they're formed and behave. In human behavior, psychologists develop theories about what motivates people by watching their behavior in different situations. In other words, we can see that some people are more motivated to read a book, and others more motivated to play a game, but knowing why isn't always easy or straightforward.

There are many theories of motivation – we've already discussed Maslow, who believed that certain needs must be satisfied – such as food and safety – before a person is interested or 'motivated' to address other needs, such as friendship and love. In the workplace, Fredrick Herzberg talks about extrinsic or external reward-based motivations – such as salary and working conditions – versus intrinsic, or internally-based motivations of achievement, recognition, and growth.

Since school is a child's workplace, we try to build motivation through external conditions such as having clean and safe environments and incentives for achieving academic goals; as well as by instilling internal rewards through the fun of learning and building attitudes of fairness and justice.

Another theory, called the expectancy theory by Victor Vroom, says that we are motivated to do well, or not, depending upon the perceived probability of success; and by the value we place upon the result, or expected reward. So if we expect to fail in a task, or if the reward for succeeding is too small or nonexistent, we may not be motivated to even try something.

Sometimes as children we've learned that we "can't do math" based on difficulty or repeated failures; and so we're not likely to try math problems, or be talked into "doing math" without a major reward. In schools we use a variety of math instructional techniques to teach kids according to their learning styles; and we use different types of rewards or incentives – certificates, trips to the zoo, tickets to a ballgame – to try to address different preferences.

In any case, with just these three theories out of many, you can see that motivation is very complex for all of us; and figuring out the best way to motivate any individual child can be difficult. But we also know that most children love to try everything, regardless of their level of skill or ability, and will often take risks for unique experiences (such as bungee jumping), or for reaching difficult goals.

It doesn't bother them to fail, even time and again, if they don't feel like someone is making fun of them or judging them in a negative way. But there are some children who are more focused on being able to perform a task well – they're less willing to take risks, and perhaps be perceived as incompetent; and may avoid failure at all costs. These differences are highly individual, and there's no research that tells us why or how these tendencies are developed. What we can do is make sure we don't penalize them, but rather challenge them to be assertive.

Solving Problems. It helps to focus on problem-solving, rather than individual abilities – kids learn by accepting a challenge, succeeding with small risks, and then moving on to bigger risks; but they need to focus on the problem at hand, rather than focusing only upon their performance level. Working in groups, especially multi-level groups, is helpful – kids learn by helping other kids, and each experiences the group (family, classroom, community) as safe and supportive. They learn to make decisions in a safe environment, and enjoy the fun of accomplishment that taking risks engenders.

Accepting Challenges. Students are motivated not only by challenging activities, but also by having fun. Initially, learning is fun to every child because they like the challenge and the new-ness of the world. Children who feel secure – safe, supported, loved, and accepted – will have "fun" taking on challenging activities that are meaningful and relevant to their own experiences. They see themselves as competent, respected, and effective; providing a basis for further risk-taking and learning.

Creating Interest. As parents, it's critical that you respect each child's different abilities, and pay attention to their interests in structuring their activities. Young children should be exposed to many different types of activities and experiences, as they (and you) learn that they like some things a lot, and others not at all.

For example, planning an activity that's in line with their interests and abilities will motivate them to read so they can learn more, and/or talk to others about their interests using "big" words that they get to explain, which enhances their social relationships. Ultimately they will want to plan their own activities, and set their own goals with your assistance and support.

Concrete Experience. Hands-on experiences are also critical. A frog is not a frog if the only place a child "experiences" it is in a book or on the internet. Pictures and words cannot convey the cold, slick feel of a frog's skin, nor realistically mimic a frog's croak or smell.

Learning words is about attaching meaning (comprehension) to our world – the meaning of the word "rose" is significantly limited if it's attached only to a picture rather than the real thing. I've read many times about how chandeliers and mirrors magnified candlelight in colonial homes, but it wasn't until I actually experienced it as an adult that I understood how effective (and beautiful) it was. The same is true with smelling roses, and having a romantic candlelight dinner.

Active Participation. Children must actively participate in doing things that are significant to them. Concrete experience also enhances interpersonal relationships – how many times have we felt an instant rapport with someone because they've actually been on the same river trip we've been on, or root for the same basketball team? This is what is motivating for all of us.

A student who is motivated will often perform at a higher level than a student who has a higher IQ, but has no interest in the problem at hand. A student may or may not test well, but nonetheless do very well in solving practical problems when interested and motivated to succeed; such as one student I worked with who had significant dyslexia and couldn't read the manual, but could perform complex, multi-level tasks on aircraft equipment when shown what to do.

Some ways in which you can help MOTIVATE your kids are:

Plan fun activities that fit their interests – storytelling at the library, visiting the zoo or a museum, or playing a game. Many museums have free days, and kids' activities.

Talk to your kids – give them a topic to discuss with you, or let them pick a topic, or simply let them talk when they're in the mood (which often results in 'I need to learn more...'.)

Be enthusiastic about events and activities – even something as simple as listening to birds in the trees or skipping rocks across a puddle.

Give them choices – some control – of what they'd like to do, and do it with them.

When they make a wrong choice, like not doing their homework, let them live with the consequences when necessary.

Connect their classroom learning to the real world – expand on what they learn in school by giving them many different types of experiences that challenge them to learn new skills, but aren't overwhelming in difficulty.

Help them feel competent as they learn new activities by encouraging – rather than simply pressuring – them to try again, maybe a different way.

Point out specific things they've accomplished – simply saying 'good job' isn't as helpful as praising the colors they've used on a map or in a drawing.

Teach them that failure is not permanent….it's simply a way of learning new things.

Chapter 23: Things You Can Do To Protect Your Children's Skin From The Harsh Sun

The more skin damage a child incurs at a young age, the more likely it is that the child will suffer from skin problems later in life, ranging from premature aging and wrinkling to skin cancer.Therefore, it is extremely important to protect your children's skin from the harsh sun's rays.The good news is that it is very easy to do so, thanks to all of the new sunscreens available to consumers that are safe and effective, even for babies.

You will want to purchase a sunscreen that has the most natural ingredients possible, as there is some research that connects the use of chemical sunscreens with skin problems.Avoid ingredients like oxybenzone and instead purchase sunscreens whose active ingredients are titanium or zinc, which are natural minerals.In this way, you avoid putting harsh chemicals on your children's skin, which could be risky.Also, be sure to use umbrellas on the beach, as well as hats if walking around in a city, for example, in order to shield the skin from the sun's direct rays.

If you can prevent burns, you reduce the chance of your child getting skin cancer.Teach your children the importance of protecting their skin, as well as the risks involved with getting too much sun exposure.While everyone needs some sun exposure in order to get enough vitamin D and be healthy, no one should overdo it.

Ways to Teach Your Children to Avoid Dangers They will Encounter Throughout Life

Children of all ages deal with peer pressure from other students at school and their circle of friends outside of school.It is important for parents to influence their children by teaching them about dangers they may encounter as they get older and showing them how to properly react to potentially frightening situations.

Drugs and alcohol can cause major problems in a child's or teenager's life, so the earlier you have a discussion about these issues with your child, the more he/she will be prepared to face the pressure to try these substances.Teach your children the dangers of these toxic substances and the proper way to avoid being forced into trying them.Tell them that people will try to convince them that these substances, including cigarettes, are not as harmful as people make them out to be, and people will also claim that they are not "cool" if they do not use these substances.If your child has enough self-confidence, he/she will not feel the need to prove anything to anyone, and he/she will be prepared to just say no to drugs and alcohol.

You should also teach your children about the consequences, including jail time and health issues, which are associated with drug, cigarette, and alcohol abuse. Give this information to your children early, because more and more children are starting to abuse these substances at younger ages. As long as you instill in them a sense of confidence and tell them how to respond to peer pressure, you can rest assured that they will be fine.

Another danger to be on the lookout for is to have children inappropriately exposed to material of a sexual nature –in their relationships with others, advertising, TV, magazines and the like. Teaching your child age-appropriate lessons in this area will help bolster them against making wrong choices in this area.

Creative Ways to Make Time to Cook More Meals at Home

Homemade meals are the absolute best way to feed your family because you can choose the freshest ingredients and make certain that you know exactly what is going into your food. By cooking homemade meals, you can rest assured that you are preparing and cooking your meals in a sanitary environment, with organic ingredients if you choose to use them, and without the need for preservatives and other additives that are found in frozen and pre-cooked meals. Frozen foods are some of the worst health offenders because they contain artificial ingredients and preservatives that can be detrimental to your family's health over time.However, you can instead prepare your meals at home and then freeze or refrigerate them for use later on.Cook large dinners so that you can be assured there will be leftovers, and then store the leftovers appropriately to retain freshness and have a lunch option for the next day or a quick snack option if one of your family member's is suddenly hungry late at night or in the middle of the day. You can also save time by cooking more than one meal at once, using most of the same ingredients in both meals.Serve one meal right away and save the other one for the next night, so that you do not have to worry about cooking dinner then.There are also many recipes available on the internet and in bookstores that offer quick meal options for the busy working mother or father who wants to be sure to provide the family with home-cooked food.

Chapter 24: Food Flying Everywhere

We often worry about our toddler's eating habits. The eating habits of our children are amongst the most common challenges that we as parents face.

Toddlers may throw food simply because they don't like the taste or they may be full. Sometimes if they see something new or something that looks colorful they may be curious enough to want to find out what it is. Or they may just want to play with it. It may be difficult for a child to express his choice of food. Some children like to eat new things and some don't. Some children like to listen to stories, watch cartoons, want a conversation while eating or may just want to eat at a certain place. We need to understand our toddler's habit, what makes them comfortable, like and dislike and accordingly set things for them.

Avoid serving large quantities and serve them in smaller portions. Once they finish their food ask them if they want more. Eventually this will also help them to learn not to waste food. Let them eat the way they want. Don't introduce another totally different food as long as they are enjoying the current one, it will allow them to taste the food thoroughly and get a good idea of what they like best, this is important especially if the food they start to like is healthy for their diet. It is ok to treat them with their favorite food once in a while but try to introduce new foods all the time, especially fruits and vegetables. You do not always have to help them eat to avoid the mess. They are small and they are bound to spill the food. Slowly let them eat on their own as they will eventually learn to eat without spilling. Try to set up time to finish the food a few minutes later if they don't finish it right away as sometimes they just get distracted but may still be a little hungry. However, if you notice your child is enjoying what he is eating even if it is taking a little long, let him finish. Don't force your toddler to eat fast.

I have seen kids who enjoy eating their food in selective utensils or plates, so let them if that encourages them to eat. My nephew eats only when he is served on his Elmo plate. See if that works for your child. It may happen that your child throws or plays with the food only when he does not like it. You need to study your child's behavior to find out the right reason. Appreciate them when they finish their food. It is alright to sometimes teach them to handle the picking up of the spilled food. Tell them to pick up the things that they throw instead of picking it up for them. Let them clean up the mess they made and praise them when they do as they will slowly learn and develop good habits from doing this.

Most people say that children should be fed at the meal time. I agree to that. However, it may be possible that there will be times when your child is not hungry and may not be able to express it. Typically, we would end up forcing them to eat assuming they are being fussy. Tell them to let you know when they are hungry and if they are not let them go.

Some children want to carry their own plates to the dishwasher or sink once they are done and that's a good habit. But we as parents tend to stop them fearing they may drop it. Don't stop them. Instead use unbreakable plate. Talking to your child and teaching them is the best way for a win- win situation.

Try some of the things you learned here but remember to give yourself and your child some time. This will all subside and get much more smoother with time and a little patience.

Chapter 25: Tips On Dealing With Parenthood

Over the last 25 years or so being a single parent has become more usual and acceptable to society. It is no longer frowned upon, in fact now days it is quite the opposite.

Many people are inspired by how they are able to look after their children alone. Over this period of time more support structures have been put in place that have help the single parent to raise their family.

Often the results of being a single parent are due to 3 main factors which are death of a spouse, divorce or a teenage pregnancy. When a child is born out of wedlock it does not in any way affect the parental status as proven by the statistics.

Over the past 20 years surveys have shown the number of single parent family households has nearly doubled. A census in America shown that 59% of children are at one stage live with a single parent. These stats are only an estimate.

Recent figures shown that there are close to 12 million single parents who are raising their family alone in the US. Adding to that figure is that children under the age of 18 will live with either their mom or dad. Just over 80% of children who live with a single mother.

The families that are headed by a single women are more vulnerable, this is because of a number of reasons. The main one being that the women's social position in society is still weaker than that of the men.

Not only do single mothers have to deal with the gender based limitations of gaining employment but also have to cope with a demanding family. This can cause a lot of pressure if she is provided with no support from external sources.

There had been policy proposals that were put in place for single parents to receive social benefits but these have been controversial. According to liberal individualist, if people choose to have children, they are responsible to look after them.

The collectivist position which dominates continental Europe holds that children are other people's business as well. This position also believes that the interest of the children is far greater than any concerns about the morality of the parents.

With people always looking for ways to cut money they often forget about the child's needs. And I'm not talking about the parent here. Being a single parent more financial support should be provided. Making sure a child grows up with the most care should always come first.

Aside from these economic realities, single parents also have to face the reality that children who live with single parents or even with a parent and step-parent, experience disadvantages in terms of psychological functioning, behavioral problems, education, and health.

Children with single parents are one and a half times likely to drop out of school and work in their early teens and twenties than children who grew up with two parents. Children with single parents are also twice as likely to have a child before the age of 20 as those raised in two-parent family.

Many psychologists and child development workers argue however that these studies are oversimplified and outdated. Many factors are involved in the psychological development of a child raised in a single parent home. Cooperation between divorced parents and quality of attention given to the child are examples.

No child in a single parent family is by default doomed for a maladjusted life. Single parents must model self-respect and self-nurturing to the children and establish a support system for the family.

Single parent surveys seem to suggest that children who live with a single parent will tend to not perform as will in their academic studies and will also receive less mental stimulation than those who live in two parent households. Personally I think the survey is false.

The best single parent advice on dealing with bringing your kids up alone would be not to be scared of asking for help from family and friends. Whether it be for babysitting or a hand in grocery shopping.

I can understand that some single parents may not have this but do not let the pressure of parenthood get to you to much. There are lots of people and information out there that will help in providing advice on what you need.

Single parents deserve our respect for being able to raise their child without a partner and should receive help in any form that they need.

Time For Potty Training

You'd be surprised that for many new parents, potty training can be something that resides on their mind from the day the child is born, messy poop disaster images can often come to mind for a new parent. Honestly, I was even kind of surprised when I got to know there are books, audios and videos for Potty Training your children, yeah I was surprised now as an experienced mother, however, now that I remember my first child especially given how young I was, I would have been one of the first to buy these potty training videos.

We start using diapers from the day our baby is born. It was mostly back in earlier times when cloth diapers were used; however they are still used today in many countries especially when cost is a factor. Can you imagine what it would be like to be using cloth diapers today? Now luckily most parents will not have to experience the hassle of hand washing these cloth diapers among other messy things.Now we have companies who have made it easier for us by introducing disposable diapers. These work really good of course. But eventually we will have to ditch the disposable diapers and have to potty train our children. Some children may learn early some may take longer.

There is no fixed rule to train you children. You keep on trying different ways and one of them will click. First and foremost you should buy plastic potties and place it in the bathroom and start talking to your child. When I was young and my nephew was very small his parents started using words like pee-pee, poo-poo to ask him if he wanted to go to the bathroom. I used to wonder how he would understand. But to my surprise after a few weeks that's how he started expressing whenever he wanted to go to the restroom. Having watched this made things easier for me when I became a mom.

Take your baby to the bathroom and tell them why they are there. You can also help them by making it a routine. In the morning when they get up, make it a habit of making them sit on the potty. It is ok if they don't get it but they will get used to it. Do not scold the child if they do it in the panties. Do not turn it into a big issue as we are talking about young little innocent children only starting to learn.It is nothing unusual and most children do it anyways, so don't feel bad about it or make a huge deal of it. Remember they will not learn this in a day. So we need to be calm and patient. If you see they are making an effort, appreciate them. If your child is not comfortable try to find out the reason. Even after making a morning routine, they may want to poo again during the day. If you notice your child is starting to quiet down and head towards a corner, or suddenly makes an urging calm face after playing around wanting to poo, pick them up and place them on the potty quickly. Once they start understanding that they need to go to the toilet or sit on the potty when they feel like "pooing", stop using diapers at least in the house. You will have to read the signs when your child needs to go. Do not force them. You may also get some books and give it to them while they are sitting on the potty, lots of parents do it.

There are various potty training ideas and techniques that we may find around. But keep in mind each child is different and if one of your children followed a specific technique or learned a certain way, it does not necessarily mean that another child will also learn to potty in the same manner. Make sure the child is comfortable and learning the right way.

Chapter 26: Keeping Cool In The Heat

Do you remember the giant from the fairy tales of your childhood? Do you remember how he would roar when he discovered there was an intruder? Are you the giant who roars to your children?

It's so easy to lose control with children...they are noisy little creatures who scurry around and get into things they shouldn't while fighting, kicking, screaming and in general, making a holy mess of things. And that's on a good day.

It's hard to believe how these dervishes can become the sweet-smelling, rosy-cheeked bundles of love that climb into your lap and look up with soft pleas for a bedtime story. The trick is to always think of them as bundles of love.

There is no question that even the most even-tempered parent has moments when they want to run. Children seem to know just how to aggravate you and when there is more than one, they coordinate their efforts to get their way. That's the point; they are trying to get their way. Why not set an example for them?

When things get tense, your body can quickly react with a fight or flight reaction. Your muscles tighten as the adrenalin is pumped into your blood system. Your breathing grows shallow and rapid. Your brain suspends all but the most necessary bodily functions as it narrows its concentration on the perceived threat. As it does this, it shuts down on rational thought and peripheral vision. Most importantly, the flood of blood and adrenalin empowers you with abnormal strength.

Obviously, this is not something you want to direct toward your child; you are literally not in control. How do you prevent this from happening? Take deep, deep breaths. Breathe deeply from your stomach, not just your chest. Not only does this give you a few moments to rationally sort out the situation, but it feeds those tensed muscles and interrupts the flight or fight impulse rushing through your system.

Postpone punishments. When you enter the living room to find your five-year-old has just used a magic marker on the grand piano keys, it feels like eternal banishment would be letting them off easily. Make a habit of delaying the sentence until emotions have cooled and reason has returned. The punishment you determine will be in proportion to the crime and therefore be respected. For the culprit there is a bit of anxiety in just imagining what their penalty will be.

Another reason you want to postpone sentencing is that you often will see the event from another perspective. The culprit may have had completely loving intentions and the transgression may have been entirely accidental. It's important to teach your children the difference between an accident and intentional misbehavior. It is simply the difference between right and wrong.

Decide who you are actually angry with. Is this aimed at the child or at yourself? Is there something else going wrong in your life or with other relationships that is actually at the root of your frustration? Learn to separate a single incident from an overall dissatisfaction. Take this opportunity to make the problems in your life go away. Address them and take a proactive stance, settle relationships, work out financial issues or go see a doctor.

Are there triggers that you already know will cause you to become angry? Avoid these triggers and learn how to walk away and moderate your reaction to those that are unavoidable. If you cannot do this on your own, get some counseling. Talk to your mate, the person who knows you best. Work out a signal that he or she can offer when it appears you are losing control. At that point, let them take over. Make it a general rule that if you are present when misbehavior occurs that the discipline is left to your mate. In other words, one person secures the area and the other determines if punishment is due.

Take the opportunity to analyze the last time a problem arose and how you handled it. It's in everyone's interest to separate discipline from emotional reaction.

Chapter 27: Enhancing Toddler Development- Fine, Gross And Visual Motor Exercises

There are many motor skills milestones that infants and toddlers will reach as they grow. If they learn in a safe and supportive environment toddlers will practice age appropriate fine, gross, and visual motor activities such as these to effectively develop. A child's overall well-being is dependent upon their development of motor skills such as stability, mobility, bilateral coordination, cognitive development, and much more.

Fine Motor Skills Activities for Toddlers

Sorting activities are a great way to practice fine motor skills with toddlers. For instance, put a number of brightly colored buttons or pompoms into a large bin then have your toddler or toddlers sort through them. One way to do this is to have them sort by color and put all the red ones in one bag, the blue ones in another bag, and so on. A slightly more advanced take on this is to have the toddlers use chopsticks to pick up the buttons or pompoms. This may be too difficult depending upon the age of your little one, but even using their fingers is an effective way to improve fine motor skills.

Another way to encourage toddlers to improve their fine motors skills is to have them lace something such as a colander. A colander is ideal because there are many holes and sometimes the holes are different sizes. A toddler should be given a piece of yarn or string then asked to create a "web" by lacing and weaving in and out of the holes. It is a fun and engaging way to keep a toddler occupied while also working on an important fine motor skill.

A great way to strengthen the hands and fingers is to complete an activity that involves pulling out small knick knacks from an egg carton. The parent or teacher can easily choose a variety of small items such as buttons or marbles then put them into the egg carton. Next, they can cut holes in the back and attach rubber bands so the toddler can pull the item towards them without removing it from the egg carton. This is a fun game to play because the parent or teacher can call out an item then the toddler must select it on their own.

Gross Motor Skills Activities for Toddlers

Gross motor skills involve more physical activity to get toddlers moving around, tire them out, and teach them to learn to move their bodies and muscles in new and different ways. One popular way to encourage the development of these skills is to have toddlers play with balloons. They should try to bat the balloons up in the air and keep them from touching the ground.

Another way to help improve gross motor skills is to create an obstacle course. This is one of the best ways for toddlers to develop because it requires them to move in many different ways. It is easy for parents or teachers to find pieces of furniture, pillows, toys, etc. to pile up in unusual ways then have kids navigate their way through. Of course, it is vital to make sure all the obstacles are safe for the children.

Using sidewalk chalk is another way for toddlers to develop gross motor skills. It is doubly effective because writing with the chalk itself helps with fine motor skill development. Creating mazes or hopscotch paths with chalk then teaching toddlers how to make their way through them is an ideal way to ensure proper gross skill development. It is fun to create specific obstacles or jumps along the way, too.

Finally, games such a Red Light, Green Light and Simon Says are perfect ways to encourage development. When playing Simon Says consider asking toddlers to move like a certain animal or a tree blowing in the wind so they can practice moving their bodies in different ways. Red Light, Green Light is also effective because it forces toddlers to learn to start and stop quickly.

Visual Motor Activities for Toddlers

There are many tasks that require toddlers to use their visual and motor skills at the same time such as drawing and cutting. One way to help them develop their visual motor skills is to have them color inside the lines. While many toddlers will scribble randomly, try to encourage them to color in a basic shape first them move on to more advanced pages from coloring books until they are able to color within the lines.

Tracing is another great way to encourage visual development. It is helpful to first have a toddler begin by tracing a line with their finger then have them use a crayon or marker to follow that same line. This is doubly effective because it also utilizes the fine motor skills necessary to hold a crayon or marker steady while completing an activity.

Popsicle sticks are great tools for working with toddlers on a variety of activities. When it comes to helping with visual motor development Popsicle sticks can be used to create letters or other shapes such as squares, rectangles, houses, and more. Show the toddler a shape first then see if he or she can recreate it using the Popsicle sticks on their own.

Finally, using beads is a good way to teach toddlers about patterns but it also effective when it comes to visual development. One great activity is to string a basic pattern then ask the toddler to copy the pattern. It is also beneficial to have them create their own pattern then attempt to recreate it as they look at it. Using different colors makes this activity more challenging and effective.

The aforementioned activities are fun ways to engage a child in play while encouraging the development of their fine, gross, and visual motor skills. Each activity is an ideal way to occupy a toddler and build a trusting relationship with them while ensuring their age appropriate development at the same time. Both early childhood educators and parents of toddlers will benefit from practicing these activities with their students or children.

Conclusion

Thank you again for downloading this book!

I hope this book was able to help you to understand why your children have tantrums and what you can do to manage them.

The next step is to put these ideas into action. Take time with your child and establish the ground rules. You can also read other informative material on the subject.

Thank you and good luck!

www.ingramcontent.com/pod-product-compliance
Lightning Source LLC
Chambersburg PA
CBHW072011070526
44583CB00015B/1431